Ea   lish

Prentice Hall Regents
Englewood Cliffs, New Jersey 07632

Library of Congress Cataloging-in-Publication Data

Malkoç, Anna Maria
    Easy plays in English / by Anna Maria Malkoç. — Rev. ed.
        p.   cm.
    Includes index.
    Contents: Marty the Martian — The television contest — Submarine
— On the bus — Sleepy head — Mr. Fix-It's repair shop — The three
singers — The opposite family — The cat in the window.
    ISBN 0–13–061698–2
    1. English language—Textbooks for foreign speakers. 2. Readers —
Drama.   I. Title.
PE1128.M334   1993
428.6'4—dc20   93–16407
                                                            CIP

Acquisitions editor: *Nancy Baxer*
Production editor: *Linda Moore*
Cover design: *Mike Fender*
Book design: *Timothy R. Waddington*
Illustrations: *David Clemons*
Pre-press buyer/scheduler: *Ray Keating*
Manufacturing buyer: *Lori Bulwin*

© **Published by Prentice Hall Regents**
Prentice-Hall, Inc.
A Simon & Schuster Company
Englewood Cliffs, New Jersey 07632

This revised edition of EASY PLAYS IN ENGLISH, first published in its original,
longer form in 1986 by Metro Kitap A.S. in Istanbul and by Wydawnictwa
Szkolne i Pedagogiczne in Warsaw, includes the first nine of the original plays in
an expanded format with new illustrations and additional preview and follow-up
language activities.

Printed in the United States of America

10   9   8   7   6   5   4

ISBN 0-13-061698-2

Prentice-Hall International (UK) Limited, *London*
Prentice-Hall of Australia Pty. Limited, *Sydney*
Prentice-Hall Canada Inc., *Toronto*
Prentice-Hall Hispanoamericana, S. A., *Mexico*
Prentice-Hall of India Private Limited, *New Delhi*
Prentice-Hall of Japan, Inc., *Tokyo*
Simon & Schuster Asia Pte. Ltd., *Singapore*
Editora Prentice-Hall do Brasil, Ltda., *Rio de Janeiro*

SPECIAL ACKNOWLEDGMENTS

The author is indebted to numerous friends in the English teaching field for inspiration and encouragement, principally to: Barbara Blackwell Gulen whose students first presented "Marty the Martian" as an experimental play at the Turkish-American Association in Ankara; Sabahat Tura, Edith Oyhon, Hikmet Malkoç, Munire Tokgoz and other colleagues in Turkey who consulted, proofread, and otherwise proved invaluable assistance on the original edition; Ewa Niezgoda, Grazyna Siedlecka, Ania Wilbik and the many dedicated teachers in Poland who provided further encouragement and support in field testing and feedback for the second edition; Jean Bodman, Donald Byrd, Allene Grognet and Dora Johnson for generously sharing their expertise and comments on format and publication; and finally and most especially to Patricia E. Matthews, the principal consultant and developer of the language practice components of this revised edition.

To all these guiding lights many, many thanks.

TABLE OF CONTENTS

FOREWORD TO THE STUDENT

Do you enjoy going to the theater?
Do you enjoy watching plays in your own language?
If you do, you will enjoy these plays for learners of English. In each play, there is a role for everyone—as an individual character, or part of a crowd, or part of the audience.

Before you begin, your teacher will help you with the introduction and preview page. You will have an idea about the play, the characters, and the special vocabulary. If possible, listen to the cassette—or to your teacher—for the pronunciation and the melody of the language.

Remember that each play is like a piece of music. Your teacher is like the orchestra conductor who helps the musicians play the pages of music. You and your classmates are like the musical instruments. When you read the pages of the play, you will bring the story to life on the stage.

After you have practiced these plays, try doing them *in your own words* in English.
I think you will enjoy the drama of the theater!

The Author

NOTES TO THE TEACHER

Purpose and Aim of the Plays

EASY PLAYS has been written especially for beginners or low-intermediate level students in English as a foreign language. They are designed to provide creative ways in which the learners can practice the language they learn in their regular English lessons. The nine plays and the accompanying language activities are not intended to comprise an "all-purpose" textbook. Rather, EASY PLAYS is a supplementary resource to enhance your usual curriculum materials. You may pick and choose the plays most suited to your students' interests and needs and easily adapt them for large or small classrooms. The language activities preceding and following each play are also adaptable in a variety of ways and involve challenging pair work and group interaction tasks.

Everyone will agree that performing a role in a dramatic play (in one's native language) is a great personal achievement. Experienced language teachers know, therefore, how highly motivating it is for their students to act out a part in a play in the foreign language. It is very much like mastering a song or a poem in the new language—a really extraordinary kind of achievement. It brings pleasure as well as increased enthusiasm and feeling for the new language. This "sweet taste of success" indeed whets the appetite for learning more!

Further, play-acting (or role-playing) is a vehicle for encouraging shy students to perform in the classroom. In these specially designed plays, there is a part for every student; the more advanced students may take the more "leading" roles, and the shyer ones may take part as voices in the crowd or members of the audience.

Grading and Levels of Difficulty

EASY PLAYS is not based on any specific textbook or curriculum. Each play is relatively simple in context and limited in the amount and level of language used. The first several plays, for example, include only simple present and present continuous verb tenses. Later units introduce the future with WILL, the future with GOING TO, and the simple past.

Vocabulary words and phrases for active mastery also are limited to the range generally found in beginning/low-intermediate level EFL textbooks. The play directions in italics include a somewhat wider range of verbs and phrases. These are not intended for active use by the students but rather for reading comprehension. The plays gradually increase somewhat in length and in complexity.

Special Features: Recycling, Repetition, Rephrasing, Group Parts

Repetition and rephrasing (or paraphrasing) occur frequently within each play. In addition, vocabulary and patterns are frequently re-introduced or "recycled" from one play to the next. This "built-in redundancy" is valuable language reinforcement for lower-level students. It reminds them of what they have learned earlier, and gives them opportunities for more practice in different situations. Overall, it helps them strengthen their mastery of the new vocabulary and structures in meaningful contexts. This extra practice is especially valuable for students who are exposed to English only within the classroom.

There is another, more theatrical purpose in the repetition and rephrasing of lines. In a stage performance, it helps the audiences catch the actors' words. Often students on stage become nervous and stage-shy. They tend to mumble and rush through their lines and drop their voices to a whisper. This makes it difficult — if not impossible— for the audience to enjoy the play. (Encouraging the students to slow down and to "project" their voices to the back row of the audience will also help this problem.)

Bracketed group parts is another special feature of EASY PLAYS. These brackets indicate the multiple voices: the people in a crowd, the audience in the TV studio, the members on the basketball teams, the animals in the farmyard, the neighbors at the birthday party, and so on. They are all saying different things to express themselves. They may all speak at once, or take turns one after the other— whatever sounds natural for the situation.

The groups have been designed to accommodate a large number of students in the classroom. It is possible to add to these groups: more people in the street, more members on the submarine crew, more passengers on the bus, and so on. In this way, all the students in the class who have not been assigned specific roles may take part in the group voices and be actively involved in the play. (They may also make up their own lines, as suitable.)

General Format of the Play Units

Each play unit contains the following pages:

- Introduction. This page consists of a general illustration, a list of the main characters, a list of key words and phrases, questions about the illustration, and general discussion questions. These provide a context and general background for reading the play.

- Preview. This page includes several vocabulary and structure exercises. These activities are designed to introduce the language in the play and to help the students feel comfortable about using it.

- Play.

- Follow-up. This page includes several more challenging activities based on the play: matching, filling-in-the-blanks, completing dialogues, interviewing, and a variety of writing tasks. These provide extra practice and reinforcement, and give the students an opportunity to express themselves creatively in their own words.

Primarily, these activities are offered as a help to busy teachers who want a few "ready-made exercises" as preparation and follow-up for each play. If you find that some activities are especially effective with one play, you can adapt them to use with other plays. Depending on the level and interests of your students, you may wish to skip these suggested activities and use your own approach for preparing and introducing the plays.

Using the Plays as Oral Language Practice

If your students are still on the lower levels, you can use these plays simply for integrated, interactive language practice. Or you may want to use them as stage productions, with your students performing them for other audiences. In either case, here are some simple introductory steps to follow:

1. First, introduce the context. Ask the students to look carefully at the illustration on the introductory page of the play and study the list of characters. Make sure they understand the general situation (as illustrated in the picture) and who the characters are. Use the suggested Questions on the Picture as a guide. Check their understanding of the Key Words and Phrases. Use the Questions for Discussion as a guide for further contextualizing the play and relating the context to their own knowledge and background.

2. Read the play aloud to the class, or play the recorded cassette tape (if one is available to you). Here you can ask the students what they understand, or do not understand. It is important that the students know the meaning of the lines before they try to practice them orally.

3. Read (or play the cassette) again, one phrase, line, or segment at a time, and have the students repeat after you all together. In this way, all of the students will read all the lines of the play together. This basic choral repetition gives the class a chance to approximate your pronunciation, stress and intonation, and phrasing by breath groups. (Practice reading the play in advance as professional radio and TV announcers do so that your oral reading is clear and smooth.)

4. Divide the class into rows or groups and assign the parts. The students read their parts silently. Then have each row or group read their parts together with you aloud. The students should try to follow your model as closely as possible. Next, ask the students to read their lines without your help.

5. Assign the individual parts to individual students when you think they are ready. Assign the group parts to rows or smaller groups. (The parts may be given as homework for the next lesson.) The individual characters perform in front of the class while the other students—the "crowds/groups/audiences/voices offstage"—perform their parts in their regular seats. This arrangement is especially advantageous in very large or crowded classrooms.

6. Rotate the parts the next time you have the students practice. This will give them a chance to read other parts for extra practice and review.

7. Ask the more advanced students to try to adapt the plays to different characters or different situations, depending on their level of ability. This can be an opportunity for additional creative expression in English.

Using the Plays for "Readers' Theater"

The "Read-and-Look-Up" technique used in readers' theater is another effective technique in addition to the group or choral reading suggestions mentioned above. Here, your students should be familiar with their lines but do not have to memorize them.

    1.Ask the students to look down while they read their lines silently.

    2.Now ask them to look up while they say their lines aloud.

In this way, the students can establish "eye contact" with the other readers in a more natural way. It is closer to real conversational dialogue than if they read their lines with their eyes glued to the book.

This kind of "expressive reading" is especially good for the shyer students; they can hold on to their books while reading their parts. This is also a wonderful opportunity for students who love to dramatize; they are free to do so while at the same time they can get support from the book if they need it.

Using the Plays as Stage Performances

As previously suggested, these plays may be used not only for group language practice or individual performances in the classroom but as theatrical performances on a stage—to show their families and friends how much English the students have learned! The presentation may include songs, dances, poems, and other dramatic numbers, with the play itself serving as a highlight of the program.

For teachers not experienced in stage productions, it is often helpful to assign some details to reliable students (rather than assigning them parts in the play). Here is a simple list of assistants and their responsibilities:

    1.Stage Manager—to prepare a check list and make sure that all of the sets, props, signs, costumes, music, special effects, and other requirements for the stage are ready and waiting for the performance.

    2.Set Manager—to be responsible for arranging the scenery and curtains and any furniture to be used on stage. In a classroom performance, the Set Manager is responsible for the pictures and drawings on the blackboard and walls and other objects for setting the scene.

    3.Props (Properties) Manager—to be responsible for special objects needed in the play. This includes things that the actors carry or use (bags, books, umbrellas, canes, baskets, etc.) and small movable pieces of furniture (tables, chairs, boxes, etc.).

    4.Sign Manager—to be responsible for preparing the signs. This includes a title sign, scene signs, a **The End** sign, and other signs that may be required. In the classroom, signs may be written on the blackboard. For the stage, they should be printed on paper that is strong enough to stand up. In either case, the signs must be large and clear enough to be read easily by the audiences.

    5.Lighting Technician—For some large school stages with elaborate lighting facilities, it may not be necessary to assign a Lighting Technician. (There are usually professional electricians to operate the stage lights.) For smaller schools, it may be possible to simply shade the windows and/or turn off the lights in the back of the room.

6. Music Technician—to help with the music (if required) and to be responsible for the musical equipment. This may consist of a tape recorder, a radio, recorded material, musical instruments, etc. The Music Technician should know the lines of the play and the clues for when the actors and scenes change.

Music, of course, adds an extra dimension to the play. Listening to music helps the audience to "bridge the gap" while the actors and/or scenes are changing. Recorded or radio music or a simple instrument played in the background (a flute or mandolin, for instance) will help fill the silence between scenes as well as set the mood for the next one.

7. Special-Effects Technician—to be responsible for all background offstage sounds that are not music. (These are indicated in the plays.) A clever Special Effects Technician can help tremendously in creating a realistic atmosphere for the play.

8. Additional Assistants—for more professional productions in a theater setting, you may also want to assign a Costume Advisor, a Make-Up Technician, a Cashier/Ticket Taker, a Publicity Manager for announcements, and/or others.

                   ᶻ᷉   ᶻ᷉   ᶻ᷉

In closing, a word for the more experienced teachers of English around the world who use EASY PLAYS. I hope these little plays and their accompanying language activities will prove to be useful innovations to add to your store of supplementary teaching materials. For the new teachers in the field, I hope EASY PLAYS will be a helpful and inspiring resource for your English language classroom. It is my sincerest wish that you and your students will all enjoy EASY PLAYS as much as I have enjoyed creating them and teaching them myself.

The Author

MARTY THE MARTIAN

Marty The Martian

CHARACTERS:

Narrator	Man	Men
Marty	Woman	Women
Old Man	Boy	Children
Narrator	Man	Men
Old Woman	Girl	

KEY WORDS AND PHRASES:

Mars	antenna	to leave	Hello!
Martian	black box	to live	Goodbye!
machine	tourist	to visit	
visitor	toy		

QUESTIONS ABOUT THE PICTURE:

1. What is in the street?   2. What is it doing?
3. Where are the people?   4. What are the people doing?

DISCUSSION:

1. Where is Mars?
2. What do you know about robots?

PREVIEW

FAMILY TREE

FILLING IN THE BLANKS WHO IS THIS?

Use the information from the Family Tree.
Examples: Who is the old man? He is the ____.
    (*He is the grandfather.*)
    Who is the girl? She is the boy's ____.
    (*She is the boy's sister.*)

1. Who is the old man? He is the ____.
2. Who is the old woman? She is the ____.
3. Who is the man? He is the ____.
4. Who is the woman? She is the ____.
5. Who is the girl? She is the boy's ____.
6. Who is the boy? He is the girl's ____.

SENTENCE BUILDING WHO ARE THESE PEOPLE? WHAT DO THEY DO?

Make complete sentences. Add your own.
Example: doctor. / work / in a hospital.
    She is a doctor. She works in a hospital.

1. doctor. / work / in a hospital.
2. mechanic. / work / in a garage.
3. secretary. / work / in an office.
4. teacher. / teach / in a school.
5. cook. / cook / in a restaurant.
6. farmer. / have animals / on a farm.
7. singer. / sing songs / on TV.
8. ____. / ____ / ____.
9. ____. / ____ / ____.
10. ____. / ____ / ____.

SENTENCE BUILDING WHO ARE THESE PEOPLE? WHAT CAN THEY DO?

Make complete sentences. Add your own.
Example: bus driver. / drive / busses. / can drive / taxis too.
    He is a bus driver. He drives busses. He can drive taxis too.

1. bus driver. / drive / busses. / can drive taxis too.
2. taxi driver. / drive / taxis. / can drive ____ too.
3. basketball player. / play / basketball. / can play ____ too.
4. football player. / play / football. / can play ____ too.
5. typist. / type / letters. / can type ____ too.
6. pilot. / fly / planes. / can fly ____ too.
7. painter. / paint / pictures. / can paint ____ too.
8. ____. / ____. / ____.
9. ____. / ____. / ____.
10. ____. / ____. / ____.

Marty the Martian

Scene: *In the street.*

Narrator: This is the street. In the street there is a bright light. Everyone—men, women, children, old men, old women—are running to look at the light. Everyone is asking questions.

Men: {
Look! Look!
Look! Look! What is it? What is it?
What is it?

Women: {
What is it?
Oh! Oh! Look!
What is it? Look! Look!
Look! What is it?

Children: {
Oh! Oh! Look! Look!
Oh! Look! Look! Oh! Oh!
Look! Oh! Oh!

Boy: Look! What is it?

Girl: What is it? Is it a toy?

Woman: A toy? A toy? H-m-m-m....

Man: A toy? No, it isn't a toy. But, what is it?

Old Woman: It isn't a toy! It isn't a girl—and it isn't a boy!

Old Man: No, it isn't a girl, or a boy, or a toy! But what **is** it?

Narrator: Everyone is looking at the light. In the light there is a black box. The box has two arms and two legs. On top there is an antenna. The box is speaking now.

Marty: Hello! Hello! Hello! What are you? What are you? What are you?

Boy: *(He is nervous.)* B-b-boy! I'm a boy! I'm a s-s-student! This is my s-s-sister!

Girl: *(She is nervous.)* H-h-hello! I-I-I'm his sister and he's my brother! I'm a student too! And this is my mother and father.

Woman: Hello! I'm their mother.

Man: And I'm their father. And this is my mother and father.

Old Woman: Hello! Hello! I'm their grandmother!

Old Man: And I'm their grandfather. What are you? Who are you?

Boy: Are you a machine?

Marty: Yes, yes, yes.
I'm a machine, a machine, a machine.
My name is Marty, Marty, Marty.
I'm a Martian, Martian, Martian.

Girl: A Martian?

Men:⎧ Listen! Listen!
⎨ He's a Martian!
⎩ Listen, he's a Martian!

Women:⎧ He's a machine!
⎨ Listen!
⎩ He's a Martian machine!

Children:⎧ Oh, oh! Listen!
⎨ Oh, listen! He's a Martian!
⎩ A machine! Oh! Oh!

Girl: Who is your mother, Marty?

Boy: Who is your father, Marty?

Marty: My mother and father? Mother and father? Mother and father?

Man: Yes, who are they? Who are your mother and father?

Marty: They're machines too! Machines too! Machines too!

Men:⎧ Machines!
⎨ Martian machines!
⎩ They're machines!

Marty: And who are you? You? You?
What are you? What are you? What are you?
I'm a typist. I can type letters.
I'm a pilot. I can fly planes.

Men and Women:
{
I'm a mechanic. I work in a garage.
I'm a doctor. I work in a hospital.
I'm a postman. I carry letters.
I'm a secretary. I work in an office.
I'm a farmer. I have sheep and cows on a farm.
I'm a cook. I work in a restaurant.
I'm a waitress. I work in a restaurant too.
I'm a bus driver. I drive busses.
I'm a basketball player. I play basketball.
I'm a teacher. I teach in a school.

Old Woman: What are you doing here, Marty?

Old Man: Yes, what are you doing here, Marty?

Girl: Are you visiting?

Marty: Am I visiting? Visiting? Visiting?
Yes, I am. Yes, I am. Yes, I am.

Men: Are you going to live here?

Women: Are you going to live here now?

Children: Are you going to live here now, Marty?

Marty: No, no, no. I'm a tourist. A tourist. A tourist.
Now, I'm going to leave here. Leave here. Leave here.

Men: Oh! Oh! He's going to leave here now.

Women: He's going to leave here. Oh! Oh!

Children: Oh! Oh! He isn't going to live here.

Boy: Why, Marty? Why are you going to leave here?
Why aren't you going to live here?

Marty: Because I can't fly. Because I can't sing. Because I can't cook.
Because I can't play basketball. Because! Because! Because!

Boy: Please don't go, Marty!

Girl: Don't go!

Men: Don't go!
Please don't go, Marty!

Women: Please don't go!

Children: Don't go!
Don't go!

Marty: No, no, no.
I'm going. Going. Going.
Goodbye! Goodbye! Goodbye!
(Marty exits.)

Narrator: Marty, the Martian machine,
waves its arms and antenna.
The bright light is very bright.
All the people close their eyes.
Then they open their eyes and
Marty the Martian isn't there!
Goodbye, Marty. Goodbye!

Everyone: Goodbye!
Goodbye!
Goodbye!

The End

FOLLOW-UP ACTIVITIES

ROLE PLAY **HELLO! WHAT'S YOUR NAME?** *Practice with a partner.*
A is Marty. B is a student. Marty asks five questions.

Example:
A: Hello! What's your name?
B: My name is _____.
A: Where are you from?
B: I'm from _____.
A: Where is _____?
B: It's _____.
A: Are you a machine?
B: ____, _____.
A: Can you _____?
B: ____, _____.

Now exchange roles. B is Marty and asks A five questions.

DIALOGUE PRACTICE *Work with your partner or in a group. Make a list of the occupations in "Marty the Martian" and add new occupations. Ask original questions.*

Examples:
A: Are you a pilot?
B: No, I'm not. I'm a student.
A: Are you a basketball player?
B: Yes, I am. And I can play football too.
A: Can you drive a bus?
B: No, I can't. But I can drive a car.

Occupations	
pilot	*Add:*
teacher	painter
student	musician
basketball player	nurse
farmer	carpenter
mechanic	banker
cook	*etc.*

WRITING PRACTICE *Write the answers to these questions in a paragraph.*

- What are the people in the street doing?
- What is Marty?
- Where is he from?
- What is he doing?
- Where is he going?
- Why is he going?

Marty

The people in the street are ____. Marty is ____.
_____.
_____.
_____.
_____.

THE TELEVISION CONTEST

The Television Contest

CHARACTERS:

Contestant Number One (a taxi driver)　　　**MC** (Master of Ceremonies)
Contestant Number Two (a train engineer)　　**Mystery Guest**
Contestant Number Three (a riverboat captain)　**Attendant**
Contestant Number Four (a bus driver)　　　**Audience**
Contestant Number Five (an airplane pilot)

KEY WORDS AND PHRASES:

transportation　　　ladies and gentlemen　　to drive
occupation / work / job　Welcome to (something)　to fly
card　　　　　　　　　　　　　　　　　　　　　to have one last chance
winner　　　　　　　　　　　　　　　　　　　　to go up and down (the river, etc.)

QUESTIONS ABOUT THE PICTURE:

1. Where are the contestants?
2. How do you know?
3. Are there more men than women? How many people are there?

DISCUSSION:

1. Is there a big television studio in your city?
2. Are there television contests in your country? Name some.
3. What do the winners receive?
4. Were you ever a contestant? Would you like to be one?

PREVIEW

PRONUNCIATION PRACTICE *Repeat the following occupations. Give more stress to the first word or syllable.*

AIRplane pilot   METro driver
HELicopter pilot   SUBway driver
TAXi driver   UNderground driver
BUS driver   RIVerboat captain
TRUCK driver   TRAIN engineer
LORry driver

DIALOGUE PRACTICE **I'D LIKE TO BE A ____.** *Work with a partner or in a group. Use some of the occupations above. Add your own.*

Example: A: Would you like to be a (*taxi driver*)?
           B: No, I'd like to be a (*helicopter pilot*).
           A: Why?
           B: Because (*I like to fly*).

FILLING IN THE BALLOONS *Work with a partner or in a group. Complete the sentences in the balloons.*

The Television Contest

Scene: *In the television studio. There is a table with six chairs and a microphone.*

The Master of Ceremonies is standing at the microphone.

MC: Good evening, ladies and gentlemen. Welcome to our program, "The Television Contest." Tonight the contest is transportation, TRANSPORTATION! We have five contestants in our contest and one Mystery Guest!
There are questions for our contestants:
Question number one: What is your name?
Question number two: Where are you from?
Question number three: What are you? or What is your job?
Then, ladies and gentlemen, there is the big question:
What is the Mystery Guest's job? Are you ready, ladies and gentlemen?

Audience: { Yes! Yes!
We're ready!
Yes! Yes!

MC: Good! Good! Ladies and gentlemen, Contestant Number One!
(Contestant Number One enters and walks to the microphone.)

C.N. One: Thank you.

MC: What is your name?

C.N. One: My name is Betty Brown, Mrs. Betty Brown.

MC: And where are you from, Mrs. Brown?

C.N. One: I'm from Texas—Dallas, Texas!

MC: Dallas, Texas? That's a famous city. A **very** famous city!
Ah, Mrs. Brown, what are you? What is your job?

C.N. One: I'm a taxi driver.

MC: A taxi driver?

C.N. One: Yes, a taxi driver. I have a taxi. I drive my taxi—in Dallas! *(The audience applauds.)*

MC: That's interesting. A taxi driver from Texas! Thank you, Mrs. Brown. *(Contestant Number One walks to the table and sits down.)* And now, ladies and gentlemen, Contestant Number Two! Welcome to our program! *(Contestant Number Two enters and walks to the microphone.)*

C.N. Two: Thank you.

MC: What is your name?

C.N. Two: My name is Harry Jones.

MC: And where are you from, Mr. Jones?

C.N. Two: Chicago. I'm from Chicago.

MC: And what is your occupation, Mr. Jones?

C.N. Two: I'm an engineer. I drive a train.

MC: A train?

C.N. Two: Yes, a train—between Chicago and New York. I'm a train engineer.

MC: I see. Very interesting. *(The audience applauds.)* Thank you, Mr. Jones. *(Contestant Number Two walks to the table and sits down.)* And now Contestant Number Three. Welcome to our program, Mr.—

C.N. Three: **Captain**! Captain Jack Green!

MC: Ah, thank you, Captain Green. And where are you from?

C.N. Three: I'm from New Orleans.

MC: New Orleans?

C.N. Three: That's right. On the Mississippi River!

MC: Ah, yes—and what is your occupation, Captain? Are you in the Army?

C.N. Three: Oh, no! I'm a pilot on a river boat on the Mississippi River. I go up and down the Mississippi River on my riverboat!

MC: That's **very** interesting. *(The audience applauds.)* Thank you, Captain. *(Contestant Number Three walks to the table and sits down.)* And now Contestant Number Four! Welcome! *(Contestant Number Four enters and walks to the microphone.)*

C.N. Four: Thank you. Thank you!

MC: Your name, please?

C.N. Four: My name's Bob—Bob Roberts! Just call me **Bob!**

MC: Ah, okay, Bob. Where are you from?

C.N. Four: I'm from Montana. Missoula, Montana. Missoula, Montana is my hometown!

MC: Oh, yes. Are you a cowboy, Bob?

C.N. Four: No. No. I'm a bus driver. I drive a big bus! In Montana!

MC: That **is** interesting. *(The audience applauds. Contestant Number Four walks to the table and sits down.)* And now Contestant Number Five, welcome!

C.N. Five: Thank you. My name is Peggy Smith.

MC: Thank **you**, Mrs. Smith.

C.N. Five: **Miss!**

MC: Miss?

C.N. Five: Yes, Miss. **Miss** Smith! I'm not married.

MC: Ah yes, excuse me. All right, **Miss** Smith, where are you from?

C.N. Five: San Francisco. I'm from San Francisco!

MC: And what is your occupation?

C.N. Five: I'm a pilot.

MC: A pilot? An airplane pilot?

C.N. Five: Yes, I have a plane, a small plane. I fly between San Francisco and Los Angeles every day.

MC: Very, **very** interesting. *(The audience applauds.)* Thank you, Miss Smith! *(Contestant Number Five walks to the table and sits down.)* Ladies and gentlemen, our contestants—five contestants—all work in transportation. Yes. A taxi driver, a train engineer, a riverboat captain, an airplane pilot, and a bus driver. And our Mystery Guest, ladies and gentlemen? What is our Mystery Guest's job? Let's see. Here is our Mystery Guest! *(The Mystery Guest enters and walks to the microphone. The audience applauds.)*

Mystery Guest: Thank you.

MC: And thank **you**, Mr. Mystery Guest! Our contestants have questions for you. Contestant Number One, please ask the Mystery Guest a **yes-or-no** question.

C.N. One: Are you from New York City, Mr. Mystery Guest?

Mystery Guest: Yes, I am.

MC: Contestant Number Two, your question, please.

C.N. Two: Are you a taxi driver?

Mystery Guest: No, I'm not.

MC: Contestant Number Three, your question, please.

C.N. Three: Are you a bus driver?

Mystery Guest: No, I'm not.

MC: Contestant Number Four, your question, please.

C.N. Four: You're not a taxi driver. You're not a bus driver. Are you a truck driver?

Mystery Guest: A truck driver—a lorry driver? No, I'm not.

MC: Contestant Number Five, the last question, please!

C.N. Five: Are you a streetcar or tram driver?

Mystery Guest: No, I'm not!

MC: All right, contestants, you have one last chance. *(She calls the Attendant.)* Attendant, please give these cards and pencils to the Contestants. *(The Attendant gives her a card and pencil to each Contestant.)* Yes, Contestants, you have one last chance! Write your answer on the card: What is the Mystery Guest's job? What is he? *(The Contestants write their answers on the cards; the Attendant takes the cards.)* And now, ladies and gentlemen, the answers! *(The Attendant gives her card number one.)* The Mystery Guest is an airplane pilot! Is that right, Mr. Mystery Guest?

Mystery Guest: No, that isn't right. That's wrong!

MC: *(The Attendant gives her card number two. She reads it.)* The Mystery Guest is a metro driver! Ah—metro is the same as subway. Are you a metro driver?

Mystery Guest: No, I'm not a metro driver or a subway driver. That's wrong!

MC: *(The Attendant gives her card number three. She reads it.)* The Mystery Guest drives an underground train. Well, ladies and gentlemen, underground train is the same as metro or subway. Am I right, Mr. Mystery Guest?

Mystery Guest: Yes, you're right. Subway, metro, and underground are the same. But I'm not a subway or metro or underground train driver!

MC: Card number four, please! *(The Attendant gives her the card. She reads it.)* Ferryboat captain. Are you a ferryboat captain, Mr. Mystery Guest?

Mystery Guest: No, I'm not. The answer is wrong!

MC: Ladies and gentlemen, our Mystery Guest is not an airplane pilot, not a subway or metro or underground train driver, and not a ferryboat captain. What is he? Card number five, please! *(The Attendant gives her the card. She reads it.)* Helicopter pilot. Are you a helicopter pilot, Mr. Mystery Guest?

Mystery Guest: Yes! Yes, I am! I'm a helicopter pilot!

MC: *(She looks at the card.)* Miss Smith, is this your card?

C.N. Five: Yes, it is!

MC: Congratulations! You are the winner of the contest! *(The audience applauds.)*

And here is one ticket for a ride in Mr. Mystery Guest's helicopter! *(She gives her a ticket.)*

C.N. Five: Oh, thank you! Thank you very much! *(She walks out with Mr. Mystery Guest; everyone applauds.)*

The End

FOLLOW-UP ACTIVITIES

ROLE PLAY **WHAT'S YOUR NAME AND WHERE ARE YOU FROM?**

Practice with a partner. A is the Master of Ceremonies. B is a Contestant.

Example:
A: What's your name and where are you from?
B: My name's _____ and I'm from _____.
A: Is _____ a famous city?
B: _____, _____.
A: Are you a _____?
B: No, I'm not a _____.
A: Last question: Then what are you?
B: I'm a _____.

Now exchange roles with your partner.

COMPREHENSION CHECK **RIGHT OR WRONG?**

If the statement is not right, correct it.

Example: There are six contestants and a Mystery Guest. *(Wrong.)*
There are **five** contestants and a Mystery Guest.

1. New York is a city on the Mississippi River.
2. The first question is: "Where are you from?"
3. Army captains usually work on riverboats.
4. A lorry driver is the same as a bus driver.
5. Another name for street car is tram.
6. A helicopter pilot works in transportation.
7. The Mystery Guest's hometown is Dallas, Texas.
8. The Mystery Guest's last name is Green.
9. The Mystery Guest asks each contestant one question.
10. The contest winner gets a helicopter ride.

WRITING PRACTICE *Imagine that the Mystery Guest is a famous singer.*

Write a paragraph about him or her. Include some of the following points:

- age
- where he/she is from
- type of music he/she sings
- who likes his/her songs
- why people like his/her music

Now read your paragraph to the group.
Can they guess the Mystery Singer?

Mystery Singer
The singer is _____ years old. _____ is from _____.
_____.
_____.
_____.
Who is this singer?

SUBMARINE

Submarine

CHARACTERS:

Narrator
Television Announcer
John Black, *an engineer*
Bill Brown, *a doctor*
Jim Cook, *an electrician*

Henry Cook, *a communicator*
Ann Smith, *a marine biologist*
Joe Smith, *a photographer*
Minnie, *a monkey*

KEY WORDS AND PHRASES:

(*submarine*) crew
engine / engineer
whale

to look at (*something*)
to be on television
to check (*something*)

Congratulations!

QUESTIONS ABOUT THE PICTURE:

1. How many people are on the submarine crew?
2. Where is Joe Smith, the photographer?
3. Who are the others and how can you tell?

DISCUSSION:

1. Have you ever seen a submarine?
2. Would you like to take a trip on a submarine? Why? / Why not?

PREVIEW

SENTENCE BUILDING **WHAT DO THESE PEOPLE DO? WHAT ARE THEY DOING NOW?** *Make sentences to answer these questions.*

Example: Ann Smith / marine biologist. look / fish.
Ann Smith is a marine biologist. She is looking at the fish.

1. Joe Smith / photographer. / take / pictures.
2. Jim Cook / electrician. / check / electricity.
3. John Black / engineer. / look / engine.
4. Bill Brown / doctor. / check / monkey.
5. Henry Cook / communicator. / talk / radio.
6. Sally Stern / TV announcer. / ask / questions.
7. Mary Benson / narrator. / introduce /story.
8. Minnie isn't a person. she / monkey. / eat / banana.

ROLE PLAY **INTRODUCTIONS.** *B introduces A to several friends. Practice with a partner.*

A: Please introduce me to your friends.
B: This is Tom Jones. He wants to be a photographer.
A: Hello, Tom. I'm glad to meet you!
B: And this is Linda James. She wants to be a doctor.
A: It's nice to meet you, Linda!
B: And this is Tim. He's an old friend. He wants to be an engineer.
A: Hi, Tim!
Now practice in a small group. Use your own names and different professions.

CHAIN PRACTICE **WHAT ARE YOU GOING TO DO TOMORROW?**

Complete the sentences. Use phrases from the list and add some of your own.

A: What are you going to do tomorrow?
B: I'm going to _____.
   And what are **you** going to do?
C: I'm going to _____.
   And what _____?
D: I'm _____.
   And _____?
E: . . . .

go fishing
take some pictures
see a movie
play
visit my _____
fly in a helicopter
eat at a restaurant
listen to the radio
watch TV
go to _____

Submarine

Scene 1: *On a street in San Francisco.*

Narrator: This is a story about a submarine.
The submarine is in San Francisco, California. It is going to San Diego, California. The submarine crew is on television now. The television announcer is asking them questions.

Announcer: Good morning, ladies and gentlemen. This is Station ABC in San Francisco, California. I am talking to Mr. John Black, engineer on the Super Submarine. Good morning, Mr. Black!

John Black: Good morning! Call me John, please!

Announcer: Okay, John! Is this your crew?

John Black: Yes, this is my crew. *(He introduces them.)*
This is Bill Brown, our doctor.
This is Ann Smith, our marine biologist.
This is Joe Smith, our photographer.
This is Jim Cook, our electrician.
This is Henry Cook, our communicator.
And this is Minnie, our monkey!

Crew:
Hello!
Hi!
How do you do!
Hi!
Hello!
Oooh! Oooh!

Announcer: Hello! It's nice to meet you! I'm glad to meet you! John, where are you going now? Are you going to the Atlantic Ocean?

John Black: No, we aren't. We're going to the Pacific Ocean—near San Diego.

Announcer: And what are you going to do?

John Black: We're going to look at fish.

Announcer: Fish? You're going to San Diego to look at **fish**? There are fish in San Francisco!

John Black: Ha-ha! We're going to look at **big** fish—and whales!

Ann Smith: Yes, white whales!

Announcer: White whales? In San Diego?

Ann Smith: Maybe. We don't know!

John Black: We're going to look at everything on the floor.

Announcer: On the floor?

Ann Smith: The ocean floor.

Announcer: Oh, I see—on the ocean floor! How long is your trip?

Henry Cook: One week.

Announcer: Well, good luck! We'll see you next week in San Diego!

John Black: Okay, thank you! Good bye!

Crew: {
So long!
Bye!
Bye!
So long!
Bye!
Oooh! Oooh!

24

Scene 2: *In the Super Submarine.*

Narrator: The Super Submarine is now in the Pacific Ocean, near San Diego. Everyone on the crew is working.
The engineer is looking at the engine.
The marine biologist is looking at the fish.
The photographer is taking pictures.
The electrician is checking the electricity.
The communicator is talking on the radio.
The doctor is checking the monkey.

Jim Cook: How's the monkey, Bill?

Bill Brown: Minnie? Minnie's fine! She's eating a banana!

Ann Smith: Hey! Look!

Joe Smith: What?

Jim Cook: What is it?

Bill Brown: Where?

Ann Smith: There! Look there!

Joe Smith: Is it a fish?

Jim Cook: Is it a whale?

Ann Smith: I don't know! I don't know **what** it is! I can't see it very well!

Bill Brown: Take a picture, Joe!

Joe Smith: I **am**! I'm **taking** a picture! Wow!

Bill Brown: Hey, John! John! Come here!

John Black: *(He enters.)* What? What is it?

Ann Smith: Look! Look!

John Black: Oh! Oh! Hey, Henry!

Henry Cook: *(He enters.)* What is it, John?

Ann Smith:
John Black: } Come here and look!

Narrator: Everyone on the crew is looking out the window. Is it a fish? Is it a whale? What **is** it? What do they see out the window?

Scene 3: *On the street in San Diego one week later. The TV announcer is interviewing the crew.*

Announcer: Well, hello! Hello! Welcome! Welcome to San Diego!

John Black: Thank you!

Crew: {
Thank you!
Thanks!
Hi!
Hello again!
Good to see you!

Announcer: Well, how are you? How was the trip?

Crew: {
Fine!
Great!
Good!
Very good!
Wow!
Fantastic!

Announcer: And the fish? The whales?

Ann Smith: Oh—no whales! No! But show the pictures, Joe! Show the pictures!

Joe Smith: Yes, please look at these pictures!

Announcer: Okay. (*She looks at the pictures.*) Oh! Is this a whale? No. No. It **isn't** a whale. Oh! Is it a ship?

Crew:
Yes! It's a ship!
It's a ship!
A Spanish ship!
Under the water!
On the ocean floor!
And old! **Very** old!

Announcer: What—What's **in** the ship? Is there anything **in** the ship?

John Black: Oh, yes! Yes, there is!

Announcer: What is it? What's in the ship?

Crew: GOLD! GOLD! GOLD!

Announcer: Gold? You mean GOLD?

Crew:
Yes! Yes!
Gold! Gold! Gold!
Spanish gold!
Three hundred years old!

Henry Cook: And here is a telegram—a telegram from the President!

Announcer: Please **read** the telegram!

Henry Cook: (*He reads.*) "To the crew of the Super Submarine: Congratulations on your good work! The President of the United States."

Announcer: Congratulations! Ah—the gold. Is some of the gold **yours** now?

John Black: Yes, it is. Half of the gold is ours.

Announcer: Wow! Congratulations! Congratulations!

Crew:
Thank you!
Thanks!
Thanks very much!
Thank you!

Announcer: But—you all get some of the gold!
How about Minnie?
What does she get?

John Black: Minnie? Oh, she gets a **bunch** of bananas!

Minnie: Oooh! Oooh!

The End

FOLLOW-UP ACTIVITIES

FILLING IN THE BLANKS *Choose the correct word from the list to complete each.
sentence.Use each word only once. Check your answers with a partner.*

1. The submarine is not _____ New York.
2. It's _____ from San Francisco to San Diego.
3. The _____ wants to look _____ fish in the Pacific Ocean.
4. In fact, they are going _____ study everything _____ the _____ of the ocean.
5. Now, near San Diego everyone on _____ crew is working.
6. The _____ is checking the engine, and the communicator _____ talking on the radio.
7. Then they _____ something big under the _____.
8. It's _____ old Spanish ship, and on it is a lot of _____.
9. The President sends them a _____ of congratulations on their _____ work.

a. floor	e. crew	i. to	m. engineer
b. good	f. see	j. water	n. is
c. going	g. on	k. an	o. gold
d. in	h. the	l. telegram	p. at

WRITING PRACTICE *Imagine that your class is taking a trip to an interesting
place in your country. Interview one of your classmates about the place and write
a dialogue. Include some of the following:*

- name of the place
- names of some of the visitors
- interesting things to see
- most unusual thing or person there
- what people are taking pictures of
- cost of the trip

Example: Interviewer: Is this your first trip to Washington, D.C.?

Classmate: Yes, it's my first visit here.

Interviewer: And who are these people with you?

Classmate: This is Miss Henderson, our teacher. Here are two classmates, Pablo Page and Mary Wilson.

Interviewer: . . . .

ON THE BUS

On the Bus

CHARACTERS:

Boy	Children	Man Number One
Girl	Mother	Man Number Two
Bus Driver	Other Passengers	Man Number Three
Old Woman		

KEY WORDS AND PHRASES:

ticket	clinic	to catch the bus	Thank you.
ticket box	hospital	to go shopping	You're welcome!
picnic basket	stadium	to point at (*something*)	
chocolate cake	traffic light	to type	
sandwiches	uniform		
restaurant			

QUESTIONS ABOUT THE PICTURE:

1. How many people are waiting for the bus?
2. What are some of them carrying?
3. Would you like to ride on this bus?   Why? / Why not?

DISCUSSION:

1. Do you ever ride on the bus? If you do, do you give your money to the driver?
2. Where do you usually get on? Where do you get off?
3. Would you like to be a bus driver?   Why? / Why not?

PREVIEW

LISTENING AND REPEATING *Repeat the following sentences after your teacher.*

1. Let's get on this bus.
2. Here's my ticket.
3. Please sit down.
4. Run! You can catch the bus.
5. Who's the man in the middle of the street?

6. Mr. Boggs will miss the bus.
7. He's too late.
8. I'm going shopping.
9. I'm getting off at the next stop.
10. I'm getting off too.

PRONUNCIATION PRACTICE *Repeat the following . Give more stress to the first word or syllable. (*Words are not in "On the Bus.")*

BUS driver	TICKet box	HOSpital stop
BUS stop	TRAFfic light	REST stop*
NOTEbook	TYPing lesson	TAXI stop*
PICnic basket		

FILLING IN THE BLANKS *Complete these sentences aloud. Choose the correct words from the list above.*

1. We put our tickets in a _____ _____.
2. We put the food for a picnic in a _____ _____.
3. The bus usually stops at a _____ _____.
4. The person who drives a bus is a _____ _____.
5. The stop for the hospital is the _____ _____.
6. The light that controls traffic is a _____ _____.
7. You use a typewriter in a _____ _____.
8. The stop to rest is a _____ _____.
9. You can find a taxi at a _____ _____.
10. You can write notes in a _____ _____.

READING PRACTICE *Read each statement aloud. If it is wrong, correct it.*

1. The bus driver takes your ticket or your money.
2. There's usually a bus stop inside every school.
3. When the traffic light is green, the bus will stop.
4. The bus driver in the picture is wearing a cap.
5. The girl in the picture wants to get off the bus.
6. There are three small children at the bus stop.
7. A policeman can stop cars and busses.
8. There's a taxi stop at every bus stop.
9. Busses between cities sometimes make rest stops.
10. The bus driver is at the back of the bus.

On the Bus

Scene: *At the bus stop and on the bus.*

Boy:	*(He speaks to the girl.)* Are you going to get on this bus?
Girl:	Yes, I am. *(They get on the bus.)*
Bus Driver:	Tickets, please. *(The Bus Driver points to the ticket box.)*
Girl:	Here's my ticket. *(She puts her ticket in the ticket box.)*
Boy:	And my ticket. *(He puts his ticket in the ticket box. Other people get on the bus.)*
Old Woman:	*(She speaks to the Bus Driver.)* Good morning! Good morning!
Bus Driver:	Good morning, Mrs. Brown. It's a nice day, isn't it?
Old Woman:	What? What? Oh, yes. Yes—nice day! *(She puts her ticket in the box and sits down.)*
Bus Driver:	*(He speaks to the Mother and Children as they get on.)* Tickets! Tickets, please. Thank you! Thank you! *(The Children and Mother speak to the Bus Driver and to each other.)* Good morning, children. Tickets, please…thank you. Tickets, tickets, please. *(The Children put their tickets in the box.)*
Children:{	We're going to the park! I have a picnic basket! I have sandwiches in my basket! And a cake! A chocolate cake! M-m-m! Chocolate cake is good! M-m-m!
Mother:	Please, children, sit down. Billy! Please sit down. That's a good boy! Sally, give me your basket. Thank you. Now, Bobby, sit here. That's fine. *(The Children sit down.)*
Man 1:	*(He speaks to the Bus Driver.)* Good morning. Here's my ticket!
Bus Driver:	Good morning, Dr. Jones.
Man 2:	*(He speaks to the Bus Driver.)* 'Morning! *(He speaks to Man 1.)* Oh, good morning, Dr. Jones! Are you going to the clinic this morning?
Man 1:	Oh, good morning, Professor Wilson! No, I'm going to the hospital this morning. *(They put their tickets in the box and sit down.)*

Other Passengers:	Good morning! Here's my ticket! And my ticket! Ticket, please.

*(The passengers give their money to the Bus Driver, take their tickets, and put them in the box. They sit down. The Bus Driver honks the horn: **Toot! Toot! Toot! Toot! Toot! Toot!** The bus is leaving now.)*

Old Woman:	Excuse me. What time is it, please?
Man 3:	It's eight o'clock.
Old Woman:	I can't hear! Please, what time is it?
Man 3:	*(He speaks loudly.)* It's eight o'clock—eight o'clock!
Old Woman:	Oh! Eight o'clock? Thank you. Thank you!
Boy:	Oh! Look! *(He points at the street.)* Look!
Girl:	What is it? What is it? What **is** it?
Children:	Mother, what is he pointing at? What **is** it, Mother?
Boy:	That man in the green suit! He can't catch the bus!
Children:	Run, run! Run! Run! Catch the bus! Run, run! Run and catch the bus! Run and catch the bus!
Old Woman:	What? What? *(She looks at the street.)* Oh! Oh! That's Mr. Boggs. Stop the bus. Stop the bus!
Man 3:	*(He speaks to the Bus Driver.)* Please, can you stop the bus?
Bus Driver:	No, I'm sorry! I can't stop the bus now.
Man 3:	*(He speaks to the Old Woman.)* He can't stop the bus.
Old Woman:	What? What? Can't he stop the bus?
Man 2:	No, he **can't**! Mr. Boggs is too late!
Old Woman:	Too late? Too late?
Man 1:	Yes, too late. *(The bus is going down the street.)*

Boy: Where are you going to go?

Girl: I'm going shopping.

Boy: What are you going to buy?

Girl: A notebook. A big notebook for my typing lessons.

Boy: Oh, can you type?

Girl: Yes, I can, but not very well. I'm learning to type.

Children:
Oh, look, Mother!
Look!
Look!

Mother: Where? Where? What is it?

Children:
Look at the man!
He's standing in the middle of the street!
See? He's stopping all the cars!
All the cars and busses and taxis!
Look!

Mother: Yes, he's the policeman. He's stopping the traffic.
The traffic light is red.

Bus Driver: Stop for the stadium. Stadium stop. Stadium stop!

Boy: I'm going to get off here. Goodbye! *(He gets off.)*

Girl: Goodbye! Goodbye!

Other Passengers:
I'm getting off here too!
Getting off here, please!

Mother: *(The traffic light is green now. The bus is going.)* Look at the street now, children. What can you see?

Children:
- I see a farmer and his horse.
- I see a pilot.

Mother: A pilot?

Children:
- Yes, a pilot in his uniform.
- And I see a waitress in her uniform.

Mother: A waitress? Where? Where is the waitress?

Children:
- Near that restaurant. See?
- And I see a nurse in a white dress.

Bus Driver: Stop for the hospital. Hospital stop!

Man 1: Here's the hospital. I'm getting off here. Goodbye!

Man 2: Goodbye!

Other Passengers:
- Getting off, please.
- I'm getting off too.
- Getting off, please. Thank you!
- Excuse me, I'm getting off!

Children: Are we getting off now, Mother?

Mother: No, not now. At the next stop. Are you ready?

Children:
- Yes, I'm ready.
- I'm ready too, Mother!
- I'm ready! *(They stand up and go to the door.* **Meeow-meeow! Meeow!***)*

Old Woman: *(She looks at their baskets.)* What's that? What's that? Is that a cat? A cat on the bus?

Bus Driver: A cat? A cat on my bus?

Mother: Children! Is that your cat? (**Meeow-meeow-meeow!**) Where is that cat?

Children:
- Oh, Mother! The little cat—
- The cat—the cat—
- Ah—ah—It's in—It's in our—basket!

Old Woman: What? What? A cat in the basket? That cat's in the basket? Ha! Ha! Ha!

Bus Driver: Stop for the park. Park stop! *(He speaks to the Children.)* Are you getting off here?

Mother: Yes, we are. Thank you!

Bus Driver: You're welcome. Goodbye, children! And—goodbye to your cat in the basket!

Children: {
Goodbye!
Thank you. Goodbye!
Bye-bye!
Meeow! Meeow!
(They get off the bus.)

The End

FOLLOW-UP ACTIVITIES

`ROLE PLAY` **WHERE DO YOU WANT TO GO?** *You meet a tourist on the bus.*
He asks you for help. In your answer use the words in the box. Add places in your
town.

Example: You: Where do you want to go?
            Tourist: To the (*train station*).
            You: This bus stops at the
                   (*train station*). Get off there.
            Tourist: How many more stops?
            You: (*Two*) more. It's (*the last stop*).

Places	
airport	park
bus station	museum
train station	the next stop
metro station	the last stop
stadium	three more stops
hospital	*etc.*

`DISCUSSION` **WHAT DO YOU THINK?** *Practice with a partner or in a group.*
Use the adjectives below or add your own. Make other changes as appropriate
and give your opinion in two or three sentences.

Example: A: All bus drivers look and act alike.
           B: All bus drivers are **different**! Some are young and some are old....

1. All bus drivers look and act alike.
   (alike / different; helpful / not helpful; careful / careless; etc.)

2. Children usually are quiet on the bus.
   (quiet / noisy, loud; polite / impolite, rude; etc.)

3. Most doctors and professors in my country ride the bus.
   (most / few; many / not many; etc.)

4. The best way to travel is by bus.
   (best / worst; most comfortable / least comfortable; etc.)

5. Cats and dogs are frequent bus travelers.
   (frequent / infrequent, rare; etc.)

6. The people on the bus are usually interesting to watch.
   (interesting / uninteresting, boring; etc.)

7. There are more people on the busses at noon.
   (more / fewer; etc.)

8. You can see more on a bus than on a train.
   (more / less; etc.)

9. It is easy to drive a bus.
   (easy / difficult, hard; etc.)

10. Most people like to ride busses.
    (most / few; many / not many; etc.)

WRITING PRACTICE *Imagine that you are on the bus with a blind friend. Your friend hears the children and asks you several questions about them. Write a short dialog between your friend (A) and you (B).*

Example: A: Who is that?
          B: Some children. They're getting on the bus.

          A: How many are there?
          B: Three—one boy and . . . .

          A: . . . ?
          B: . . . .

Now describe the children in a paragraph or two. Include most of the following information:

- how many children there are
- their names and ages
- what is in the baskets
- what they can see from the bus
- where you think they will get off
- where you think they are going
- several things you think they will do in the park

Example: A mother and her young children are getting on the bus. . . .

SLEEPY HEAD

Sleepy Head

CHARACTERS:

Narrator
Mrs. Harris, *the mother*
Mr. Harris, *the father*
Polly Harris, *the daughter*
Fred Harris, *the son*
Mr. Macdonald, *the basketball coach*
Voices *(offstage)*

KEY WORDS AND PHRASES:

star *(player)*	to dream	Hooray!
to be awake	to be on time	That's too bad!
to be in bed	to be ready *(for something)*	I'm very sorry.
to get out of bed	to play *(in the Olympics)*	Wait a minute.

QUESTIONS ABOUT THE PICTURE:

1. Where are the people in the picture? 2. What are they doing?
3. Where is Fred? 4. What is he doing?

DISCUSSION:

1. Do you remember your dreams?
2. Do you usually have good dreams or bad dreams?
3. Can you describe one of your dreams?

PREVIEW

VOCABULARY PRACTICE *How many words can you substitute for the underlined words? Work with a partner and make a list. Repeat the sentences with the new words.*

tea/pot
milk
water
food
bread
eggs
magazine
letter
telegram
lunch
dinner
etc.

Example: Mr. Harris sits down for (*breakfast*). (*lunch, etc.*)
1. Mrs. Harris puts the (*coffee pot*) on the table.
2. Then Polly pours the (*coffee*).
3. Everyone eats (*breakfast*) silently.
4. Mr. Harris reads his (*newspaper*) while he eats.
5. Mrs. Harris carries Fred's (*breakfast*) to the (*dining room*).
6. Mrs. Harris picks up the (*sugar*) from the table.

LISTENING AND REPEATING *Repeat the following sentences after your teacher. Then practice with a partner.*

A: Good morning, Dad.
B: Good morning, Polly.

A: I'm hungry. It's time to eat.
B: Here's your breakfast.

A: Thank you.
B: You're welcome.

A: I'm late. Goodbye!
B: Bye, Dad!

A: I'm sorry. Fred's not here.
B: That's too bad!

A: Poor Fred! He's still sleeping.
B: Yes, what a sleepy head!

DESCRIBING **BREAKFAST AT YOUR HOUSE.** *Tell what some of these people do at breakfast at your house.*

Example: My mother cooks the eggs. She cuts the bread.
Then she calls my father. . . .

- You
- Your mother
- Your (younger / older) sister
- Your (younger / older) brother
- Your father
- Your wife / husband
- Your grandmother / grandfather
- Other people

Sleepy Head

Scene 1: *The dining room of the Harris home.*

Narrator: This is the dining room of the Harris home.
Mrs. Harris, the mother, is putting breakfast on the table.
(Mrs. Harris enters, puts the coffee pot on the table.)
Polly, the daughter, helps her mother. *(Polly enters, and puts plates, cups, and saucers on the table.)* Mr. Harris, the father, comes in with the morning newspaper. *(Mr. Harris enters. He is reading the newspaper.)*

Mr. Harris: Good morning! Good morning! *(He sits down.)*

Polly: Good morning, Dad! *(She puts food on the table.)*

Mr. Harris: *(He is still reading the newspaper.)* Breakfast is ready?
Of course. Ah, good. Good! I'm hungry! Where are the children? *(He starts to eat.)*

Polly: I'm here, Dad! *(She pours the coffee.)* Here's your coffee. Sugar? *(She puts sugar in his cup, then she sits down.)*

Mr. Harris: Oh. *(He looks up.)* Oh! Yes, yes, of course! Thank you, Polly. *(He drinks his coffee.)* Ah, yes. Now, where is Fred?

Mrs. Harris: Fred? Fred is sleeping, dear. *(She sits down at the table.)*

Polly: He's a sleepy head!

Mr. Harris: Sleeping? Oh! Yes, yes, of course! *(Everyone eats breakfast silently.)* What time is it, Polly?

Polly: It's eight o'clock, Dad!

Mr. Harris: Eight o'clock! Oh! Oh! *(He gets up.)* I'm late! Goodbye, goodbye. I'm going to the station! *(He exits quickly.)*

Polly: Goodbye, Dad!

Mrs. Harris: Goodbye, dear!

Polly: And I'm going to the library, Mother. *(She picks up the plates, cups and saucers from the table and exits.)*

Mrs. Harris: All right, dear. Goodbye! *(She picks up the coffee pot and food from the table and exits.)*

Narrator: And where is Fred, the sleepy head? Still in bed? Yes, Fred is sleeping. Fred is dreaming. This is Fred's dream . . . .

Scene 2: *The school.*

Fred: *(He enters. He is wearing his pajamas.)* Oh, oh! I'm late! I'm late! *(He looks around.)* This is my school—but where is Mr. Macdonald, our basketball coach? Where is the basketball team? Where is the **basketball**? Where are my **friends**?
(He walks slowly around the room. Then he goes to the chair in the corner and sits down. He closes his eyes.)

Voices: *(Offstage)* { Fred! Fred! The Sleepy Head!
Fred! Fred! The Sleepy Head!
Get out of bed! Get out of bed!

Mr. Macdonald: *(He enters. He is carrying a large clock.)*
What time is it? What time is it? Is everyone here today?
Where is the girls' team? The girls' team? *(He looks outside.)*

Girls' Voices: *(Offstage)* { Here!
Present!
Present!
Here, Mr. Macdonald!

Mr. Macdonald: And the boys' team? Is the boys' team here?

Boys' Voices: *(Offstage)* { Present!
Right here!
Here, Mr. Macdonald!

Mr. Macdonald: Good! Good! *(He looks at the clock.)* Both teams are here today. Very good! And both teams are in the Olympic Games today! IN THE OLYMPIC GAMES!

Voices: {
Hooray!
Yeah! Yeah!
Hooray! Hooray!
Hooray! Hooray! Hooray!

Mr. Macdonald: Are you ready, teams? Are you all ready for the Olympics?

Voices:
(Offstage) {
Ready! Ready!
We're ready, Mr. Macdonald!
Yes sir! We're all ready for the OLYMPICS!
The girls' team is ready!
The boys' team is ready!

Mr. Macdonald: Good! **Very** good! But—wait a minute! Wait a minute! Where is our best player? Our best player isn't here! Where is our STAR? WHERE IS FRED HARRIS? *(He looks around. He listens to the voices offstage.)*

Voices:
(Offstage) {
He's still in bed, Mr. Macdonald!
He's still sleeping!
Fred! Fred! the Sleepy Head!
Fred! Fred! He's still in bed!
Freddy, Freddy, we're all ready!
Where are you? You? You?
Poor Freddy! Never ready!

Mr. Macdonald: Oh! That's too bad! I'm sorry! No Olympics! No Olympic Games today! I'm very sorry! *(He exits slowly. Then Fred stands up and exits slowly.)*

Scene 3: *The dining room of the Harris home.*

Narrator: Yes, poor Fred! That was a bad dream! But now Fred is awake. Here he comes into the dining room.

Fred: *(He enters. He is carrying his school books.)* Mother? Dad? *(He looks around.)* Polly? Where **is** everyone?

Mrs. Harris: *(She enters. She is carrying Fred's breakfast.)* Good morning, Fred!

Fred: Good morning, Mother! *(He sits down and eats his breakfast.)* What time is it?

Mrs. Harris: *(She sits down and drinks a cup of coffee.)* Oh, it's ten minutes after eight. Your father is at the station—and Polly is at the library.

Fred: Ten minutes after eight? Ten minutes after **eight**? *(He eats quickly and stands up.)*

Mrs. Harris: Where are you going, Fred?

Fred: I'm going to school, of course. Today I'm not late! Today I'm on time. *(He picks up his books and goes to the door.)* Today our team is playing in the Olympics! Good-bye. *(He exits quickly.)*

Mrs. Harris: The Olympics? The Olympics? Fred, are you dreaming? *(She goes to the door and looks out.)* Fred? Fred? The Olympics? He's dreaming! *(She shakes her head. She picks up the dishes and shakes her head again.)* Today is Saturday! There's no school today, Fred! *(She exits quickly off-stage.)* Fred? Fred?

The End

46

FOLLOW-UP ACTIVITIES

ROLE PLAY IT'S 7:30. WHERE'S FRED? HE'S LATE!

Fill in the blanks for places in the box. Then practice this telephone conversation with a partner. Use the information from the box and add your own words.

Mr. Macdonald:	Good morning, Mrs. Harris.
Mrs. Harris:	Good morning, Mr. Macdonald.
Mr. Macdonald:	It's (7:30). Where's Fred? He's late!
Mrs. Harris:	He's (*still in bed*).
Mr. Macdonald:	What's he doing?
Mrs. Harris:	He's (*sleeping*).
Mr. Macdonald:	He's sure a sleepy head!

Time	Place	Activity
7:30	in bed	sleep
7:45		dream
8:01		wake up
8:03	in the bedroom	get up
8:05		get dressed
8:10		eat breakfast
8:16	at the door	leave (for school)

MATCHING FRED HARRIS LIKES TO PLAY BASKETBALL.

Work with a partner. Find the places for these sports. Add other sports to your list. Then make a sentence for each one.

Examples: 1. playing basketball (e.)
Fred Harris likes to play basketball on the basketball court.

6. running (b.)
Fred Harris likes to run in the park.

1. playing basketball
2. playing football (soccer)
3. playing tennis
4. playing table tennis (ping pong)
5. playing _____

6. running
7. skating
8. skiing
9. swimming
10. _____ ___

a. down the mountain
b. in the park
c. in the stadium
d. in the lake
e. on the basketball court
f. on the ice
g. on the table
h. on the tennis court

WRITING PRACTICE *Work with a partner or in a group. Use information from lists A, B, and C and the matching exercise above (and/or add your own words) to complete this news story.*

A. Sport
boxing
diving
gymnastics
ice hockey
running
skating
skiing
swimming
tennis
wrestling
etc.

B. Person
boxer
diver
gymnast
h. player
runner
skater
skier
swimmer
t. player
wrestler
etc.

OLYMPIC GAMES

Yuri Zuri, the great Olympic 1.(A) star, is going to the Olympic Games in 2.(C) tomorrow. Yuri says, "The Games are fantastic!" He likes 3.(A) in the winter in 4.(C) and 5.(A) in the summer in 6.(C). Yuri is 7.(age) years old and lives in 8.(C). He is the finest 9.(B) in the world today. Bravo, Yuri! We'll see you in 10.(C)!

C. Place
Australia
Brazil
Canada
France
Germany
Italy
Japan
Norway
Sweden
USA
etc.

MR. FIX-IT'S REPAIR SHOP

Mr. Fix-It's Repair Shop

CHARACTERS:

Narrator
Mr. Nelson, *an old man*
Mrs. Nelson, *an old woman*
Mr. Fix-It, *the repairman*

Mrs. Smith, *first customer*
Mr. Jones, *second customer*
Miss Brown, *third customer*

KEY WORDS AND PHRASES:

to fix
to come back
to put on (*coat, etc.*)
to wind up (*clock, etc.*)
to turn on/off (*TV, etc.*)
to pick up

broken (*radios, etc.*)
refrigerator
eye glasses
on the radio

It doesn't work.
Oh, darn it!
What's your problem?
Good idea!

QUESTIONS ABOUT THE PICTURE:

1. What do you see in the picture?
2. Where are Mr. and Mrs. Nelson?
3. What are they doing?

DISCUSSION:

1. Do you have anything that doesn't work? If you have, describe it.
2. Do you ever go to a repair shop? Why? / Why not?

PREVIEW

DIALOGUE PRACTICE MY WATCH DOESN'T WORK.

Practice the conversation below with a partner. Substitute the underlined words with words in the box. Add your own.

Example: A: Oh! Oh! My <u>car</u> doesn't work.
               B: Take it to a repair shop. They'll fix it.

watch	bicycle
clock	computer
radio	lamp
car	typewriter
TV	*etc.*

CHAIN PRACTICE TURN ON THE TV. / TURN IT ON.

Practice these conversations in a group. Use the words in the box and add your own.

Example: A: Please turn on the (*TV*).
               B: All right, I'll turn it on.
                     Please turn on the (*light*).
               C: All right. I'll turn it on.
                     Please turn on the ____.
               D: . . . .

TV	gas
fan	motor
light	lamp
radio	water
computer	electric typewriter
	etc.

CHAIN PRACTICE TURN OFF THE TV. / TURN IT OFF.

Practice these conversations in a group. Use the words in the box above and add your own.

Example: A: It's time to go. Let's turn off the (*TV*).
               B: Okay. I'll turn it off.
                     It's time to go. Let's turn off the (*light*).
               C: Okay. I'll turn it off!
                     It's time to go. Let's ____.
               D: . . . .

FILLING IN THE BALLOONS ONE, I'M FIRST. TWO, I'M SECOND . . . .

1.	first
2.	second
3.	third
4.	fourth
5.	fifth
6.	sixth
7.	seventh
8.	eighth
9.	ninth
10.	tenth

Number off from one to ten around the class, several times if necessary. Practice the numbers with a partner or in a group. Then fill in the balloons.

Mr. Fix-It's Repair Shop

Scene 1. *In the Nelson home.*

Narrator: Mr. Fix-It is a repairman. He fixes everything: broken radios, televisions, refrigerators, automobiles, clocks, watches—everything! Now, Mr. and Mrs. Nelson have a radio. It doesn't work. They are going to take the radio to Mr. Fix-It.

Mr. Nelson: Mary! Mary! Where are my glasses? *(He looks for his glasses.)*

Mrs. Nelson: Why, Harold, they're on the table.

Mr. Nelson: And where is my notebook? *(He looks for his notebook.)*

Mrs. Nelson: It's on the table too, dear.

Mr. Nelson: Thank you. And where is my new pen? *(He looks for his pen.)*

Mrs. Nelson: I don't know, dear. Maybe it's on the radio.

Mr. Nelson: H-m-m-m. . . . Where is my pen? *(He looks at the radio.)* Oh, Mary, what time is it now?

Mrs. Nelson: It's time for the news, dear.

Mr. Nelson: Good. Let's listen to the news. *(He turns on the radio. It doesn't work.)* Mary, this radio doesn't work!

Mrs. Nelson: It doesn't work?

Mr. Nelson: No, it doesn't. Oh, darn it! I always listen to the news on this radio.

Mrs. Nelson: I know, dear. You **always** listen to the news on the radio.

Mr. Nelson: Well, I **like** this radio. I like the **news** on this radio.

Mrs. Nelson: I know, dear. Harold, let's take the radio to Mr. Fix-It!

Mr. Nelson: Good idea, Mary. Let's take it **now**!

Mrs. Nelson: All right, dear. Just a minute. I'll put on my coat. *(They put on their coats and exit.)*

Scene 2. *At Mr. Fix-It's repair shop.*

Narrator: Mr. and Mrs. Nelson go to Mr. Fix-It's repair shop. They take the radio and give it to Mr. Fix-It. He is sitting at his repair table. *(Mr. and Mrs. Nelson enter.)*

Mr. Nelson: Good morning!

Mrs. Nelson: Good morning!

Mr. Fix-It: Good morning! *(He smiles.)* What's your problem?

Mr. Nelson: It's our radio. It doesn't work!

Mr. Fix-It: Oh? Let's turn it on. *(He turns it on.)* You're right. It doesn't work. *(He turns it off.)*

Mrs. Nelson: It's very old. . . .

Mr. Nelson: It's forty years old!

Mr. Fix-It: Forty years old? *(He looks at the radio carefully.)* Y-e-e-e-s, I see. It **is** very old!

Mrs. Nelson: Can you fix it?

Mr. Fix-It: I don't know. Come back on Saturday.

Mr. Nelson: Saturday? Okay. Thank you very much.

Mrs. Nelson: Goodbye!

Mr. Nelson: Goodbye!

Mr. Fix-It: Bye! See you Saturday! *(Mr. and Mrs. Nelson exit.)*

Scene 3: *At Mr. Fix-It's repair shop one week later.*

Narrator: It is Saturday. Mr. and Mrs. Nelson want to pick up their radio. They go back to Mr. Fix-It's repair shop. There are many people in the shop.

Mr. Fix-It: All right. Who is first, please?

Mr. Jones: I'm first.

Mrs. Smith: No, I'm first!

Miss Brown: That's right. She's first! *(She points to Customer 1.)* And he's second. *(She points to Customer 2.)* And I'm third!

Mr. Fix-It: Okay, okay! *(He smiles at all the customers. Then he looks at Customer 1.)* Good morning, Mrs. Smith!

Mrs. Smith: Good morning!

Mr. Fix-It: Here's your clock, Mrs. Smith. *(He winds it up.)* Now, it works! *(He gives the clock to Customer 1.)*

Mrs. Smith: Thank you very much! *(She pays Mr. Fix-It and exits.)*

Mr. Fix-It: Next, please!

Mr. Jones: I'm next!

Mr. Fix-It: Yes. Good morning, Mr. Jones. *(He smiles at Customer 2.)*

Mr. Jones: Good morning!

Mr. Fix-It: Here's your watch. *(He winds it up.)* Now it works! *(He gives the watch to Customer 2.)*

Mr. Jones: Good. Thank you! *(He pays Mr. Fix-It and exits.)*

Mr. Fix-It: Next, please.

Miss Brown: Good morning!

Mr. Fix-It: Good morning. Miss Brown, here is your television. *(He turns it on.)* Now it works! *(He gives the television set to Customer 3.)*

Miss Brown: Oh, good! Thank you very much! *(She pays Mr. Fix-It and exits.)*

Mr. Nelson: Good morning!

Mrs. Nelson: Good morning!

Mr. Fix-It: Good morning! *(He smiles.)* Are you next?

Mr. Nelson: Yes, we are. We want our radio.

Mr. Fix-It: Your radio. Well, here is your radio.

Mrs. Nelson: Does it work now?

Mr. Nelson: I always listen to the news on the radio.

Mr. Fix-It: Well, I'm sorry—

Mr. Nelson: Sorry? Sorry?

Mrs. Nelson: Doesn't it work?

Mr. Fix-It: No, it doesn't. It's very old. But—

Mr. Nelson: Can't you fix it?

Mr. Fix-It: No, I can't. But—will you sell it?

Mrs. Nelson: Sell it?

Mr. Nelson: Sell my radio?

Mr. Fix-It: Yes, **sell** it. The museum wants to buy it.

Mr. Nelson: The museum? The museum wants to **buy** my radio?

Mrs. Nelson: How much will the museum pay?

Mr. Fix-It: Five hundred dollars.

Mr. Nelson: Five hundred dollars? Okay. Okay! *(Mr. Fix-It pays him the money.)*

Mrs. Nelson: Good. Good! Now let's buy a **new** radio. I want to listen to the news on a **new** radio!

Mr. Nelson: All right.Thank you! Goodbye!

Mrs. Nelson: Goodbye!

Mr. Fix-It: *(He smiles.)* Goodbye. Goodbye! *(Mr. and Mrs. Nelson exit.)*

The End

54

FOLLOW-UP ACTIVITIES

FILLING IN THE BLANKS **WHERE TO GO/WHAT TO PICK UP.**

Complete columns 1 and 2. Work with a partner and add your own words.

Example: *(library)* / a book

1.	2.
repair shop	our radio
_____	a book
_____	two theater tickets
_____	some medicine
post office	_____
_____	my sick friend
_____	two bus tickets
_____	a notebook
flower shop	_____
eye doctor	_____
_____	_____
_____	_____

ROLE PLAY **LET'S PICK UP OUR RADIO.**

Make up a role play with your partner. Use information from the box above.

Example:　A:　What time is it now?
　　　　　　　B:　It's *4:30*. It's time to go!
　　　　　　　A:　Go where?
　　　　　　　B:　Let's go to the __ and pick up ___.

MATCHING **EXPRESSIONS.** *Choose an expression from the box below to follow each sentence. Use each expression only once.*

Example: Here's your camera. I fixed it. *(Now it works.)*

1. Here's your camera. I fixed it. _____.
2. The museum will pay me for my old car. _____.
3. Mr. Fix-It's shop is full and I'm late. _____.
4. I know you like this old clock but I can't fix it. ____.
5. Nobody will buy this old refrigerator. _____.
6. So, you want to take the clock to Mr. Fix-It. _____.
7. It seems to me that this watch works. _____.
8. I can't see the TV. ____.

a.	Good idea!
b.	It doesn't work.
c.	I need my glasses.
d.	Darn it!
e.	Good!
f.	I'm sorry.
g.	What's the problem?
h.	Now it works.

WRITING PRACTICE *Write a paragraph describing a good Mr. / Mrs. Fix-It that you know. Include some of the following information about the person.*

- who he/she is *(friend, relative, shop owner)*
- where he/she works *(in a shop, in a garage, at home, etc.)*
- what he/she can fix *(lamps, clocks, cars, washing machines, clothes, dishes, etc.)*
- what he/she is like *(patient, careful, mechanical, quiet, friendly, fast, on time, prompt, etc.)*
- whether the work is cheap/expensive
- why people like him/her

THE THREE SINGERS

The Three Singers

CHARACTERS:

Rooster	**Narrator**
Donkey	**Other Animals** (*off stage*)
Cat	**Robbers** (*off stage*)

KEY WORDS AND PHRASES:

farmyard	hungry	to go someplace	Get out of the sack!
farmhouse	sleepy	to wake up	Indeed!
suitcase	tired	to kill (*someone*)	Help! Help!
voice	musical	to go back	

QUESTIONS ABOUT THE PICTURE

1. Who are the three important animals in the picture?
2. Where are they?
3. What is the rooster carrying?
4. Which animals are not leaving the farmyard?

DISCUSSION:

1. This play is based on the old story "The Three Musicians of Bremen." Do you know this story? What happens in the story?
2. Are there many of these animals in your country? Which ones?
3. Which animal would you like to be in this play? Why? / Why not?

PREVIEW

DIALOGUE PRACTICE DO YOU SEE ANY FOOD? I'M HUNGRY!

Work with a partner. Make questions and answer them. Use the words in the box and add your own.

Examples: A: Do you see any *(food)*? I'm *(hungry)*!
B: Yes, there's some *(food)* on the table.
A: Do you see any *(water)*? I'm *(thirsty)*!
B: No, I'm sorry. There isn't any. . . .
A: Do you see any _____? I'm _____!
B: Yes, _____.
A: Do you see any _____? I'm _____!
B: No, _____.

Nouns	Adjectives
food	
bread	
rice	hungry
meat	
fruit	
water	
tea	
coffee	thirsty
lemonade	
etc.	

SUBSTITUTION PRACTICE WHAT A BEAUTIFUL VOICE!

Work with a partner. Substitute the underlined words with words in the box. Add your own.

Examples: What a *(beautiful/voice)*!
What an *(expensive/radio)*!

Now form sentences in the plural.

Examples: What *(beautiful/voices)*!
What *(expensive/radios)*!

Adjectives	Nouns
beautiful	animal
enormous	boy
expensive	building
famous	car
fantastic	computer
fat	girl
great	man
hungry	movie
musical	radio
sleepy	story
tall	submarine
thin	trip
etc.	*etc.*

The Three Singers

Scene 1: *In the farmyard.*

Narrator: This is an old story about three animals,
three musical animals: a rooster, a donkey, and a cat. Each
animal has a beautiful voice—or thinks it has a beautiful
voice! The animals are unhappy in the farmyard.
They want to leave. They want to go and sing in the Big City,
where everyone will hear their beautiful voices.
This morning the first musical animal, Mr. Rooster,
is in the farmyard. He is carrying a suitcase.

Rooster: Cock-a-doodle-doo! Cock-a-doodle-doo! (*He walks up and
down the farmyard.*) Oh! My voice is beautiful! My voice is
very beautiful this morning! Cock-a-doodle-doo! Do-o-o-o!
(*The other animals are offstage.*)

Hen: Cluck! Cluck! Cluck! Time to get up! Cluck! Cluck!

Cow: Moo! Moo! Good morning to you! Moo! Moo! Moo! Moo!

Duck: Quack! Quack! Quack! Get out of the sack! Quack! Quack!

Dog: Bow-wow! Bow-wow! Wake up now! Wake up now!
Bow-wow! Bow-wow!

Cat: Mew-mew! Mew-mew! Good morning to you! Meow! Meow!
Mew! mew!

Donkey: Hee haw! Hee haw! See saw! See saw! Hee Haw! Hee haw!
(*He comes in and sees the Rooster.*) Good morning, Mr.
Rooster! (*Then he sees the suitcase.*) Oh! What is that?

Rooster: This? (*He holds up his suitcase.*) This is my suitcase.

Donkey: I see. Are you going someplace? Are you leaving, Mr. Rooster?

Rooster: Yes, yes, I am! I'm leaving. I'm going to the Big City.

Donkey: To the Big City, Mr. Rooster? Why are you going to the Big
City? Why are you leaving the farmyard?

Rooster: Oh, Mr. Donkey, this farmyard is small, very small for **me**! I
have a beautiful voice—cock-a-doodle-doo! Cock-a-doodle-doo!
And I'm going to sing in the Big City!

Donkey: Yes, Mr. Rooster, your voice is beautiful. Very beautiful! And **my** voice is beautiful too! Listen! Hee-haw! Hee-haw! Hee-haw! Hee-haw! My voice is beautiful too!

Rooster: Yes! Yes! You have a **beautiful** voice, Mr. Donkey. Come to the Big City with me. We can sing together. Cock-a-doodle-doo!

Donkey: Hee-haw! Hee-hee-hee-haw! (*The Donkey goes to get his suitcase.*)

Narrator: So, Mr. Donkey goes to get his suitcase. The two friends are going to go to the Big City together. But before they leave, Mrs. Cat comes along.

Cat: (*She enters and sees the Rooster and the Donkey. They are carrying their suitcases.*) Oh! Oh! Meow! Meow! What now? What now?

Rooster: Good morning, Mrs. Cat!

Donkey: Good morning, Mrs. Cat!

Cat: (*She points to their suitcases.*) What's that? And that?

Rooster: Our suitcases, Mrs. Cat.

Donkey: Suitcases!

Cat: Are you two leaving? Are you going to go someplace?

Rooster: Yes, we are! Cock-a-doodle-doo! We have beautiful voices! This farmyard is too small for us. We're going to the Big City. We're going to sing in the Big City! Cock-a-doodle-doo!

Donkey: Listen to our voices, Mrs. Cat. Hee-haw! Hee-haw! He-e-e-e!

Rooster: Cock-a-doodle-doo! Do-o-o-o! Do-o-o-o!

Cat: Oh, Mr. Rooster! Mr. Donkey! Your voices are **beautiful**. Very, **very** beautiful! And my voice—my voice is beautiful **too**. Listen to my voice! Mew-mew! Meow! Meow! Mew-mew! Meo-o-o-o-w!

Rooster: Indeed! Indeed, Mrs. Cat! What a beautiful voice! Come with us to the Big City. We can sing together!

Cat: Oh, yes! Yes! Yes! Meow. Meow. Tra-la-la! Tra-la-la! (*She runs out and comes back with her suitcase.*)

Narrator: Mrs. Cat goes to get her suitcase. The three friends say goodbye to their friends in the farmyard. *(The Rooster, the Donkey, and the Cat wave goodbye to the other farmyard animals.)*

Rooster: Goodbye! Cock-a-doodle-doo! Cock-a-doodle-doo! Goodbye to you!

Donkey: Hee-haw! Bye-bye! Hee-haw! Bye-bye!

Cat: Meow! Meow! Mew-mew! Goodbye to you! Meow! Meow! Mew-mew! Goodbye to you! *(The three friends slowly exit. The other animals are all off stage.)*

Hen: Good luck! Cluck! Cluck! Good luck!

Duck: Hurry back! Quack! Quack! Hurry back!

Cow: Moo! Moo! Moo! Moo! Goodbye to you!

Dog: Bow-wow! Bow-wow! They're leaving now!

Scene 2: *On the road.*

Narrator: So the three friends go along the road to the Big City. They walk along . . . and walk along . . . and walk along. Now it is night and they are very tired. They see a farmhouse on the road. *(The three animals enter slowly.)*

Donkey: Oh, I'm **tired**! Hee . . . Haw . . . .

Rooster: Oh, I'm tired! And **hungry**! Cock- a-doodle . . . do-o-o . . . .

Cat: Oh, I'm tired! And hungry! And **sleepy**! Meow. . . M-m-m. . . .

Rooster: *(He looks up and sees a farmhouse.)* Oh! Look! Look! Cock-a-doodle-doo! Look! Look!

Cat: What? Meow! What is it?

Donkey: Hee-haw! What? What? What?

Rooster: There! There! See? There's a farmhouse! *(The Rooster points.)* There's a light in the window!

Cat: No—no! I can't see! *(The three animals go to the window.)* Can you see in the window, Mr. Donkey?

Donkey: *(He looks in the window.)* Yes—yes! I can see! Ooooh!

Narrator: The Cat and the Rooster are too short to look in the window, but the Donkey is tall. He looks in the window and sees three men. They are sitting at a table counting money. Each man has a large bag of money and he is counting his gold!

Rooster: *(He whispers loudly.)* Mr. Donkey! Mr. Donkey!

Donkey: Sh-h-h-h-h! Sh-h-h-h-h!

Rooster: What do you see in there, Mr. Donkey?

Donkey: *(He whispers loudly.)* I see three men . . . .

Rooster: Do you see any food? Do you see any **food**? I'm **hungry**, Mr. Donkey!

Cat: Yes, we're hungry, Mr. Donkey! Mew-mew!

Donkey: Sh-h-h-h-h! Sh-h-h-h-h!

Cat: Do you see any **beds**, Mr. Donkey? I'm **sleepy**!

Donkey: No, no. I don't see beds or food! There are three men and— *(He looks in the window again.)* They are counting MONEY! MONEY! MONEY!

Rooster: MONEY!

Cat: MONEY!

Donkey: Yes, bags of money! Oh-h-h-h! Oh-h-h-h!

Rooster: H-m-m-m! I have a plan, Mr. Donkey, Mrs. Cat . . . .

Cat: A plan? A plan, Mr. Rooster?

Donkey: A plan? What **is** it?

Rooster: Yes, I have a plan. Let's sing! Let's **sing** for them! *(He points to the window.)* We have beautiful voices—

Cat: Yes! Yes! **Beautiful** voices!

Donkey: Yes, let's sing! And then? And then?

Rooster: And then, the men will give us MONEY for singing!

Donkey: And food? Food? I'm hungry!

Cat: And a bed? I'm sleepy!

Rooster: I don't know! Mrs. Cat, Mr. Donkey—please! Let's sing!

Cat: All right! Let's sing!

Donkey: Okay! Okay! Let's **sing**!

Rooster: One—Two—Three—Cock-a-doodle-doo! Hello to you!

Cat: Mew-mew! Hello to you!

Donkey: Hee-haw! Hee-haw! Hee-haw! Hee-haw!

Rooster: Cock-a-doodle-doo! Hello! How do you do! Do-o-o-o!

Cat: Meeow! Meeow! We're singing now! Meeoow!

Donkey: Hee-hee! Hee-hee! I see you three! I see you three! He-e-e-e!
(The three friends smile happily and exit.)

Robbers: *(Offstage)* Listen! Listen! What is it? What is it?
Oh! Oh! Oh! Help! Help!
They're going to kill us! They're going to kill us!
Police! Police! Help! Help! *(There is the sound of the robbers running away.)*

Scene 3: In the farmyard.

Narrator: And so, dear friends, the Robbers heard the three musical animals—Mr. Rooster, Mr. Donkey, and Mrs. Cat—and they ran away! Yes, they ran away and they are still running. Our three singers took their bags of money and went back to the farmyard. *(The three animals come back on stage. They are carrying three bags of money.)*

Rooster: Cock-a-doodle-doo! Cock-a-doodle-doo! Good morning to you!

Cat: Meow! Meow! We're happy now! So happy now!

Donkey: Hee-haw! Hey, hey! What a beautiful day!

Rooster:
Cat: } Hey, hey!
Donkey: Hey, hey!
What a **beautiful** day!

The End

FOLLOW-UP ACTIVITIES

MATCHING **BILINGUAL ANIMALS.** *Work with a partner or in a group. Make a list of animals and what they "say" in your own language. Then match the animals in Box 1 with what they "say" in English in Box 2. Add as many animals as you can.*

1.	2.
cat _____	a. Cock-a-doodle-doo!
cow _____	b. Hee-haw! Hee-haw!
dog _____	c. Quack! Quack!
donkey _____	d. Moo! Moo!
duck _____	e. Meow! Meow!
hen _____	f. Bow-wow! Bow-wow!
rooster (cock) _____	g. Cluck! Cluck!
etc.	*etc.*

SCRAMBLED SENTENCES *Work with a partner or in a group. Unscramble the sentences below and write them down. Then read them to your partner or group.*

Example: and / hungry / The / was / rooster / cat / the / was / . / sleepy

The cat was sleepy and the rooster was hungry.

1. / . / in / animals / sang / the / The / City / three / never / Big
2. and / . / hens / cow / a / dog / a / lived / the / also / farmyard / Two / , /, / in
3. do / they / voices / beautiful / , / ? / Roosters / have / don't
4. suitcases / I / carry / to / heavy / . / like / don't
5. isn't / big / cat / donkey / A / a / . / is / and / strong / but
6. on / live / Do / ? / farm / city / or / a / in / you / a
7. streets / the / are / cities / there / cats / In / . / on / many / some
8. and / the / . / away / robbers / The / ran / animals / heard / three
9. of / money / carried / The / farmyard / friends / to / singing / the / . / the / bags
10. happy / . / robbers / were / the / were / singers / The / unhappy / but

WRITING PRACTICE *Write a paragraph about your favorite animal (or pet), or a famous animal you have known. Include some of the following information:*

- name
- kind of animal
- color, size, age
- personality (*friendly, quiet, noisy, etc.*)
- why it is different from others
- why you like or dislike the animal

You might begin like this: "I'm never going to forget _____."

or: "_____ was a famous _____."

THE OPPOSITE FAMILY

The Opposite Family

CHARACTERS:

Narrator

Mrs. Opposite

Mr. Opposite

Neighbors

Billy Black, *a neighbor*

Timmy

Jimmy}*twin sons of Mr. and Mrs. Opposite*

Policeman

KEY WORDS AND PHRASES:

birthday cake	delicious	to knock (*at the door*)	Congratulations!
birthday candle	opposite	to look for (*something*)	Excuse me.
birthday party	twins	to lose (*something*)	Happy birthday!
birthday present	downstairs	to make a mistake	Many happy returns of the day!
surprise	upstairs		

QUESTIONS ABOUT THE PICTURE:

1. Who is bringing in the cake?
2. What is on top of the birthday cake?
3. Who will cut the cake?
4. Does Timmy look like Jimmy?
5. How old do you think they are?

DISCUSSION:

1. How do you celebrate your birthday?
2. Name several special things you or your family do on your birthday or on a special day.
3. Do all twins look alike?

PREVIEW

VOCABULARY PRACTICE OPPOSITES. *Fill in the blanks with the opposite words. Add pairs of opposites of your own.*

upstairs	-	downstairs	happy	-	_____	to lose	-	_____
big	-	small	short	-	_____	to open	-	_____
black	-	_____	asleep	-	_____	to go	-	_____
awful/ugly	-	_____	thin	-	_____	to turn on	-	_____
new	-	_____	old	-	_____	_____	-	_____
good	-	_____	Hello!	-	_____	_____	-	_____

CHAIN PRACTICE WHAT'S THE OPPOSITE OF ____?

Work in a group. Use the words in the box above and add pairs of your own.

Example: A: The opposite of **upstairs** is **downstairs**. What's the opposite of **big**?
B: The opposite of **big** is **small**. What's the opposite of **awful**?
C: The opposite of **awful** is ____. What's the opposite of ____?
D: ____. ____?
E: ....

ROLE PLAY HAPPY BIRTHDAY, JOHN!

Practice with a partner. Give true information about yourself.

Example: A: Happy birthday, John! Congratulations!
John: Thank you. When's YOUR birthday?
A: It's on ____.
John: How old will you be?
A: It's a secret! Did you get any nice birthday presents today?
John: My Mom gave me a photo album. What do you want for your birthday?
A: I'd like a new ____.

Now exchange roles with your partner.

The Opposite Family

Scene: *An apartment in the Green Apartment Building.*

Narrator: We are in the home of the Opposite Family. They live in apartment number four in the Green Apartment Building. Today is Jimmy's and Timmy's birthday. They are thirteen years old. Their mother, Mrs. Opposite, is bringing a birthday cake to the table now.

Mrs. O: *(She enters and stands at the door.)* Surprise! Surprise! Happy birthday, Timmy! Happy birthday, Jimmy!

Jimmy:
Timmy: Oh, look! A birthday cake! Thanks, Mom! *(Mrs. Opposite puts the cake on the table and sits down.)*

Mr. O: It's beautiful!

Jimmy:
Timmy: It **is** beautiful, Mom! Thank you!

Mr. O: *(He smiles at his sons.)* Today you are thirteen years old. *(He pulls packages out of his pocket.)* Here's a surprise for you, Jimmy! And a surprise for you, Timmy!

Jimmy:
Timmy: Oh, **thanks**, Dad! Thank you very **much**!

Mr. O: *(He laughs.)* Happy birthday! And now, open your birthday surprises. *(They open the packages.)*

Jimmy:
Timmy: Oh, thanks, Dad! Thanks very much!

Mrs. O: Jimmy, please bring plates for the cake—and knives and forks!

Jimmy: Okay, Mom! *(He gets up and goes out to the kitchen.)*

Narrator: The birthday cake is a surprise and the birthday presents are a surprise. And now, another surprise—a policeman is at the door! *(There is the sound of knocking at the door.)*

Mr. O: Who is that? Who is knocking at the door? *(He gets up and goes to the door. He opens it.)*

Policeman: Good afternoon! *(He has a notebook and pencil in his hand. He is very polite.)*

Mr. O: Good afternoon! *(He is very surprised.)*

Policeman: Mr. Black?

Mr. O: No, my name's Opposite.

Policeman: Oh. You're Mr. White?

Mr. O: No, I'm not. Mr. White is downstairs.

Policeman: Mr. White is downstairs? *(He looks at his notebook.)*

Mr. O: Yes, Mr. White is **downstairs**—and Mr. Black is **upstairs**!

Policeman: Mr. Black is upstairs? *(He looks at his notebook.)*

Mr. O: Excuse me. Who are you looking for?

Policeman: I'm looking for a thirteen-year-old boy. *(Timmy gets up and goes to the door.)*

Timmy: **I'm** thirteen years old!

Policeman: **You're** thirteen years old? *(He looks at his notebook.)* What's your name, please?

Timmy: Timmy. My name's Timmy. *(The policeman writes the name in his notebook. He writes slowly and carefully.)*

Mrs. O: *(She goes to the door.)* Please come in! *(She looks at Timmy.)* Timmy, please bring another plate—and knife and fork!

Timmy: All right, Mom! *(He goes out to the kitchen. Jimmy comes back in from the kitchen. He is carrying four plates, knives, and forks. He stops and looks at the policeman.)*

Mrs. O: *(She speaks to the policeman.)* This is a birthday party! Please sit down and have some birthday cake!

Policeman: Well, ah—thank you very much! *(He sits down at the table. Then he looks at Jimmy.)* Ah, now, Timmy, you're thirteen years old today?

Jimmy: Excuse me, my name isn't Timmy.

Policeman: *(He looks at his notebook.)* Your name isn't Timmy?

Jimmy: No, sir. It's Jimmy.

Policeman: Oh—sorry. I made a mistake. *(He corrects the notebook.)* Jimmy! *(He smiles at Jimmy.)* All right now, Jimmy! You're thirteen!

Jimmy: Yes, sir. That's right. *(He smiles at the Policeman.)* I'm thirteen! *(He puts the four plates, knives, and forks on the table.)*

Mrs. O: Jimmy, please bring a big knife for the cake!

Jimmy: All right, Mom! *(He goes out to the kitchen. Timmy comes back in with one plate, knife, and fork. He puts them at the policeman's place at the table. Then he sits down.)*

Mr. O: Thank you, Timmy!

Policeman: *(He is writing notes in his notebook. He is surprised.)* Timmy? Timmy? *(He looks at his notebook.)* Isn't your name Jimmy?

Timmy: No, sir. My name's Timmy! *(Jimmy comes back in with a big knife for the cake. He puts it on the table and sits down.)* His name's Jimmy! *(Everyone laughs. The surprised Policeman laughs, too.)*

Policeman: Oh, I see! You're twins!

Jimmy:
Timmy: } Yes, we're twins! Today is our birthday!

Policeman: Well, happy birthday, Jimmy! Timmy! *(He looks at his notebook again.)* I'm looking for a thirteen-year-old boy.

Mr. O: Why?

Mrs. O: Yes, why are you looking for a thirteen-year-old boy?

Policeman: Because we have his dog! *(He reads from his notebook.)* "Mr. Smith down the street found a small dog. The dog was with a boy from the Green Apartment Building. The boy was thirteen years old."

Mr. O:
Mrs. O: } The Green Apartment Building? That's **our** building!

Jimmy:
Timmy: } But we don't **have** a dog!

Mrs. O: What color is the dog?

Policeman: *(He looks at his notebook.)* Brown. The dog is brown. What color is the Blacks' dog?

Mr. O: I don't know.

Mrs. O: Mr. **White** has a dog.

Policeman: And the Whites live upstairs?

Mr. O: No, the **Blacks** live upstairs. The Whites live **downstairs**.

Policeman: *(He looks at his notebook.)* Oh, yes! Is the Whites' dog **white**?

Mrs. O: No, it's **black**. *(The Neighbors knock at the door.)* Excuse me. Someone is at the door. *(She goes to the door and opens it.)* Oh, hello! Hello! *(The Neighbors are standing at the door.)* Please come in. Hello! Come in, come **in**! *(The Neighbors enter. They are carrying birthday presents. They give their presents to Jimmy and Timmy.)*

Neighbors: {
Happy birthday, Jimmy and Timmy! Congratulations!
Many happy returns of the day!
Happy birthday, boys!
Congratulations, Timmy! Jimmy!

Jimmy: }
Timmy: } Thank you! Thank you very much! Thanks!
(They shake hands with each Neighbor.)

Mrs. O: Please sit down. Please sit down. *(Some Neighbors sit down. Some Neighbors help Mrs. Opposite. They bring in more plates, knives and forks, and tea cups from the kitchen. She gives cake and tea to everyone.)* Cake? Tea? *(Some Neighbors help her.)*

Neighbors: {
Yes, please. Thank you!
Yes, please. Thank you very much!
Oh, yes, please. Thanks!
M-m-m-m! Good! Very good cake!
Delicious! Delicious cake!

Mr. O: *(He sees the neighbor boy, Billy Black.)* Oh, look! This is our neighbor, Billy Black. He lives upstairs.

Policeman: *(He looks at his notebook.)* Ah, yes. Hello, Billy! *(He smiles at Billy.)* How old are you, Billy?

Billy: I'm thirteen years old.

Policeman: Do you have a dog, Billy?

Billy: Yes, sir. Ah—no, sir. I lost my dog.

Policeman: Lost? You **lost** your dog? What **color** is your dog, Billy?

Billy: Brown. It was brown.

72

Policeman: *(He smiles at Billy.)* I found your dog, Billy. It's downstairs—in my car!

Billy: Downstairs? In your car? Oh! Oh! Let's go! Let's **go**! *(He shakes hands with Jimmy and Timmy.)* Thanks for the birthday party. Bye, Jimmy. Bye, Timmy. Happy birthday!

Policeman: Thank you for the birthday party. Goodbye.

Mr. O: Goodbye, Billy! *(He speaks to the policeman.)* You're welcome!

Mrs. O: Goodbye.

Jimmy: }
Timmy: } Thank you! Goodbye! *(The Policeman and Billy exit.)*

The End

FOLLOW-UP ACTIVITIES

MATCHING **BIRTHDAY PARTY.** *Work with a partner. Select the best response for B from the list in the box. Use each response only once.*

1. A: Please sit down and have some birthday cake, sir.
   B: _____

2. A: The twin's birthday cake is a surprise. I made it myself.
   B: _____

3. A: Jimmy, please bring a plate for the policeman.
   B: _____

4. A: Today we're thirteen years old.
   B: _____

5. A: Good afternoon. I'm looking for Mr. Black.
   B: _____, but I'm Mr. Opposite.

6. A: You'll have some birthday cake and tea?
   B: _____

7. A: My name isn't Timmy. It's Jimmy.
   B: _____

8. A: Here's a surprise for you, Timmy.
   B: _____

a. Happy birthday!
b. Sorry, I made a mistake.
c. Thank you very much.
d. Sorry
e. All right, Mom.
f. Thanks, Dad!
g. It's delicious cake!
h. Yes, please.

WRITING PRACTICE *Read the dialogue below. Then do the exercise on the next page.*

A: I went to a terrible party last night.

B: Really! Tell me about it.

A: First, I didn't know anybody at the party.

B: That's too bad! How was the music?

A: It was so-so. The singer didn't have a good voice and the band played poorly. I didn't dance at all.

B: What was the food like?

A: It wasn't very good. The fish and the rice were so-so. The coffee was weak and the cake was awful!

B: I guess you didn't have a good time.

A: No, I didn't. And the weather was bad too. I walked home in the rain.

B: I'm glad I didn't go to that party!

74

Now work with a partner or in a group. Take the opposite point of view and rewrite the dialogue. Use some of the adjectives in the box and add your own.

Example: A: I went to a fantastic party last night.

B: Really! Tell me about it.

A: First, I knew a lot of people at the party.

B: Great!

A: . . . .

delicious
fresh
tasty
wonderful
great
beautiful
fantastic
fine
good
lovely
excellent
marvelous
etc.

THE CAT IN THE WINDOW

The Cat in the Window

CHARACTERS:

Narrator
Mr. Moto, *the antique dealer*
Tour Guide
Tourists

Archeologist 1
Archeologist 2
Archeologist 3

KEY WORDS AND PHRASES:

antique	plan	to be disappointed	Good luck!
antique dealer/shop	problem	to be interested in	See you later!
tour guide/group	shake	to buy/sell *(something)*	So long!
tourist	in front of	to be for sale	
bottle	in the corner	to pay *(money for something)*	
bowl	broken	to talk about *(something)*	
box/boxes	lovely		

QUESTIONS ABOUT THE PICTURE:

1. Where is Mr. Moto?
2. Who are the people in front of the antique shop?
3. What is for sale in the shop windows?

DISCUSSION:

1. Are there any antique shops in your city or town? What can you buy there?
2. Do you or your family have any antiques? How old are they?
3. What kind of antiques do you like to look at in a museum?

PREVIEW

SENTENCE BUILDING A DOCTOR'S A PERSON WHO ____.

Work with a partner. Make complete sentences.

Example: doctor / person / take care of / sick people
A doctor's a person who takes care of sick people.

1. antique dealer / person / sell / valuable old objects
2. tourist / someone / like / travel / interesting places
3. tour guide / man or woman / take care / tour groups
4. archeologist / person / study / old places / things
5. narrator / someone / tell / story / about characters / play
6. Mr. Moto / dealer / own / antique shop
7. pilot / person / fly / planes or helicopters
8. driver / person / drive / car, taxi, bus or truck
9. actor / someone / like / role play
10. cat / animal / like / drink / milk

Now change your sentences to plural. (In 2, 5, and 9, change someone *to* people; *in 6, change* Mr. Moto *to* Mr. and Mrs. Moto.)

Example: Doctors are people who take care of sick people.

DIALOGUE PRACTICE MAY I LOOK AT ____, PLEASE?

Practice with a partner. Use the information in the box. Use the correct singular/plural forms.

Example: A: May I look at the (*tall bottle*) in the window, please?
B: Sorry, it's not for sale!
A: Then, may I look at these (*big boxes*)?
B: Sorry, they're not for sale!

Adjectives	Nouns	Phrases
tall	bottle	in the window
short		on the table
small	bowl	in the corner
interesting		on the floor
pretty	box	under the table
big		near the _____
_____		next to the _____

78

The Cat in the Window

Scene: *In an antique shop.*

Narrator: Mr. Moto was an antique dealer who owned a small antique shop. He always had a lot of interesting antiques in the window of his shop. And there was always a cat who sat in the window and drank milk from an old bowl. Tour groups liked to visit Mr. Moto's shop and look at his antiques. One morning, a tour group stopped in front of Mr. Moto's window.

Tour Guide: And this is Mr. Moto's antique shop.

Tourists: { Oh, look at all the **antiques!**
What lovely **bottles**!
I like the small **blue** bottles!
And I like the tall **green** ones.
Look at the cat in the window!
What a pretty cat!

Mr. Moto: Good morning! Good morning!

Tourist: Good morning! Hello!

Mr. Moto: Do you want to look at antiques?

Tourists: { Yes, I want to look at the tall green bottles, please.
May I look at the blue bottles, please?
How much are the little cups?
How much are those boxes?
How much are these bowls?

Narrator: The tourists talked to Mr. Moto about the antiques. He sold them bottles, cups, boxes, and bowls. They paid him and left. *(The tourists exit.)* Then two men came along the street. They were archeologists and they were interested in antiques. They stopped in front of the shop.

Archeologist 1: Oh, this is Mr. Moto's shop!

Archeologist 2: Yes. He has some interesting antiques, hasn't he?

Archeologist 1: Yes, he has. H-m-m-m, those bottles are very interesting!

Archeologist 2: Say, look at that old bowl!

Archeologist 1: Which old bowl?

Archeologist 2: The old bowl in the corner. The **cat's** bowl!

Archeologist 1: Oh, yes, I see it! The cat's drinking milk from it. H-m-m-m, it **is** very interesting.

Archeologist 2: And very **antique**! Come on, let's ask Mr. Moto about it!

Archeologist 1: Okay, let's ask him.

Narrator: So the two archeologists entered the shop. They wanted to ask the antique dealer about the cat's bowl.

Mr. Moto: Good morning. Come in. Come in!

Archeologist 1: Good morning!

Archeologist 2: Good morning! Ah, we saw the cat's bowl in the window.

Mr. Moto: The cat's bowl?

Archeologist 1: Yes, the cat is drinking milk out of it.

Mr. Moto: Oh, **that** bowl! That's just an old bowl. It's old and broken.

Archeologist 2: Well, **we** like it.

Archeologist 1: Yes, we **like** it. We—ah, we like the **color**.

Archeologist 2: Yes, we like the color! And—ah, the **shape**! How much **is** it?

Mr. Moto: How much is it? Oh, I'm sorry. That bowl's not for sale!

Archeologist 1: Not for sale?

Archeologist 2: You won't sell it?

Mr. Moto: No, I won't sell it. It's not for sale. Sorry!

Narrator: So the two archeologists didn't buy the bowl. They were disappointed, of course. As they left Mr. Moto's shop and walked down the street, they saw their friend Jim. *(The two archeologists walk out of the shop and stop in front.)* He was also an archeologist.

Archeologist 3: *(He enters.)* Hello, Jack! Hello, Bob!

Archeologist 1: ⎫ Hello, Jim!
Archeologist 2: ⎭

Archeologist 3: You look unhappy! What's the problem?

Archeologist 1: We were in Mr. Moto's shop.

Archeologist 2: We wanted to buy an antique bowl.

Archeologist 1: It's very old and **very** interesting.

Archeologist 2: But he wouldn't sell it to us!

Archeologist 3: Which bowl **is** it?

Archeologist 1: It's the cat's bowl in the corner.

Archeologist 2: See? The cat's drinking milk from it. *(They point to the bowl in the window.)*

Archeologist 3: Ah, yes. I see it. H-m-m-m, it **is** very interesting. And I think I have a plan.

Archeologist 1: A plan to buy it?

Archeologist 3: Yes.

Archeologist 2: Well, good luck!

Archeologist 1: Yes, good luck! *(They both laugh.)* So long! Goodbye!

Archeologist 2: Good-bye! See you later!

Archeologist 3: Right! See you later! *(The two men leave; the third man enters the shop.)*

Mr. Moto: Good morning! May I help you?

Archeologist 3: Ah, good morning. I—ah, was looking at your cat.

Mr. Moto: My cat?

Archeologist 3: Yes, your cat in the window.

Mr. Moto: Oh, yes, of course! My cat in the window.

Archeologist 3: I **love** cats.

Mr. Moto: Yes, cats are interesting animals.

Archeologist 3: Yes, they **are**. Yes! I—ah, love cats very much and I want to buy a cat.

Mr. Moto: You want to **buy** a cat?

Archeologist: Yes.

Narrator: So Mr. Moto and the archeologist talked about cats—and about Mr. Moto's cat in the window. Finally, Mr. Moto said he would sell his cat to the archeologist for one hundred dollars!

Archeologist 3: All right, Mr. Moto, here is your money! *(He counts it out.)* One hundred dollars.

Mr. Moto: Thank you! *(He takes the money)* And here is your cat!
(He takes the cat out of the window and gives it to the archeologist.)

Archeologist 3: Thank **you**! Thank you **very** much! *(He starts to leave, but stops at the door.)* Oh! Ah—by the way . . . .

Mr. Moto: Yes?

Archeologist 3: Ah. I—ah, don't have a bowl for the cat's milk . . . .

Mr. Moto: No bowl?

Archeologist 3: No, I have no bowl for the cat's milk. But—I'll buy the cat's bowl in the window.

Mr. Moto: The cat's bowl?

Archeologist 3: Yes, the old, broken bowl. How much is it?

Mr. Moto: Oh, sorry! It's not for sale!

Archeologist 3: Not for sale?

Mr. Moto: No. You see, because of that bowl I sell a lot of cats!

The End

FOLLOW-UP ACTIVITIES

PUZZLE THE ANTIQUE SHOP. *Work with a partner or in a group to solve* this crossword puzzle.

Across

1. very old valuable things
5. opposite of NEAR
6. opposite of OUT
8. opposite of FROM
9. opposite of LAW
10. a flower
11. opposite of LITTLE
13. a dealer who loves cats
15. K L M ___ ___ P Q R
16. abbreviation for Los Angeles (California)
17. opposite of COMING
19. a package or something to put things in
21. to start
22. male child
23. opposite (feminine) of GENTLEMAN
24. opposite of BEGINNING
26. where the cat likes to sit
27. read and _____

Down

1. the study of very old things
2. a short interesting trip
3. what tourists ask
4. what the cat is doing in the window
7. opposite of YES
9. the place where we live
12. opposite of COME
14. a car we pay to ride in
18. 3 x 3 = ?
19. what we sleep in at night
20. a color
21. abbreviation for Buenos Aires (Argentina)
23. not high
25. a negative

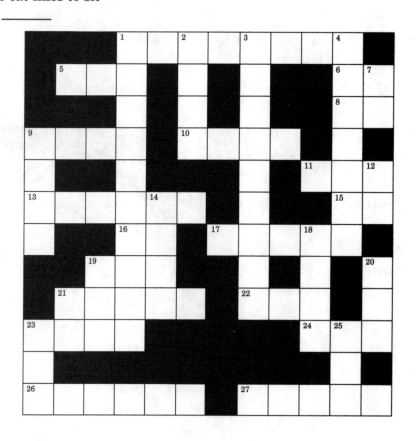

WRITING PRACTICE *Work with a partner to complete your own ending to "The Cat in the Window." Choose one of the sentences below and then write your ending in four or five sentences in dialogue form.*

- Archeologist 3 pays more money for the cat and gets the bowl.
- Archeologist 3 buys the shop in order to get the bowl.
- Mr. Moto agrees to sell only the bowl—for **lots** of money.
- Your own idea.

Example:

Archeologist 3:	Good morning. I'd like to buy that cat in the window.
Mr. Moto:	Why do you want my cat?
Archeologist 3:	It's a beautiful cat. How much is it?
Mr. Moto:	H-m-m-m . . . .
Archeologist 3:	Well, I . . . .
Mr. Moto:	. . . .

Index of Key Words and Phrases

KEY TO QUESTIONS AND EXERCISES

MARTY THE MARTIAN
Questions about the Picture (*some possible responses*) p 2
  1. A black box./ There is a black box in the street.
  2. It is talking to the people./ It is looking at the people.
  3. People./ People are in the street./ There are many people in the street.
  4. They are looking at the black box./ They are talking to the black box./ They are asking questions.

Preview: Filling in the Blanks p 3
  1. grandfather
  2. grandmother
  3. father
  4. mother
  5. sister
  6. brother

Sentence Building: Who Are These People? What Do They Do? p 3
  1. She is a doctor. She works in a hospital.
  2. He is a mechanic. He works in a garage.
  3. She is a secretary. She works in an office.
  4. She is a teacher. She teaches in a school.
  5. He is a cook. He cooks in a restaurant.
  6. He is a farmer. He has animals on a farm.
  7. She is a singer. She sings songs on TV. *etc.*

Sentence Building: Who Are These People? What Can They Do? p 3
  1. He is a bus driver. He drives busses. He can drive taxis too.
  2. She is a taxi driver. She drives a taxi. She can drive cars too.
  3. He is a basketball player. He plays basketball. He can play football too.
  4. He is a football player. He plays football. He can play tennis too.
  5. She is a typist. She types letters. She can type books too.
  6. He is a pilot. He flies planes. He can fly helicopters too.
  7. She is a painter. She paints pictures. She can paint boxes too. *etc.*

Follow-Up Activities: Writing Practice (*some possible responses*) p 8
(The people are) looking at Marty./ They are talking to Marty.
Marty is a Martian./ Marty is a robot.
He is from Mars./ He is from the planet Mars.
He is talking to the people./ He is visiting./ He is looking at the planet Earth.
He is going back to Mars./ He is going to return to Mars./ He is going home.
He is going because he is not happy./ He is going because he can't fly or sing or cook or play basketball./ *etc.*

THE TELEVISION CONTEST
Questions About the Picture (*some possible reponses*) p 10
1. In a TV studio./ They are at a TV studio table.
2. Yes, there are seven. / There are four men and three women.
3. I / we know it's a TV studio because it has a TV camera and a microphone./ I see a TV camera./ It has a TV camera./ There are people in the audience./ *etc.*

Preview: Filling in the Balloons p 11
1. Hello! My name's Betty Brown. I'm a taxi driver. I drive a taxi.
2. Hello! My name's Harry Jones. I'm a train engineer. I drive a train.
3. Hello! My name's Jack Green. I'm a pilot/ captain on a river boat. I go up and down the Mississippi River.
4. Hello! My name's Bob Roberts. I'm a bus driver. I drive a big bus.
5. Hello! My name's Peggy Smith. I'm a pilot. I fly a small plane.

Follow-Up Activities: Comprehension Check: Right or Wrong? p 18
1. Wrong. (*New York City is on the Hudson River; New Orleans is on the Mississippi River.*)
2. Right.
3. Wrong. (*Riverboat captains/ pilots work on riverboats; army captains work in the army.*)
4. Right.
5. Right.
6. Right.
7. Wrong. (*The Mystery Guest's hometown is New York City.*)
8. Wrong. (*We don't know the Mystery Guest's last name.*)
9. Wrong. (*The Mystery Guests answers one question from each contestant./ Each contestant asks the Mystery Guest one question.*)
10. Right.

SUBMARINE
Questions about the Picture (*some possible responses*) p 20
1. Six./ There are six people on the crew./ Six people and one monkey.
2. In the middle. He's between the communicator (*with the headphones*) and the doctor (*in the white coat and with the stethoscope*).
3. The TV announcer is the woman on the left; she has a mike in her hand. Ann Smith is the biologist; she is the only other woman. Bill Brown, the doctor, is in the back behind Ann Smith; he is wearing a white coat and has a stethoscope. John Black, the engineer, is probably the man in the white coat in front; he is talking to the TV announcer. The man behind John Black, looking at the TV announcer, must be Jim Cook, the electrician.

Preview: Sentence Building: What Do These People Do? What Are They Doing Now? p 21
1. Joe Smith is a photographer. He is taking pictures.
2. Jim Cook is an electrician. He is checking the electricity.
3. John Black is an engineer. He is looking at the engine.
4. Bill Brown is a doctor. He is checking the monkey.
5. Henry Cook is a communicator. He is talking on the radio.
6. Sally Stern is a TV announcer. She is asking questions.
7. Mary Benson is a narrator. She is introducing the story.
8. Minnie isn't a person. She's a monkey. She is eating a banana.

Follow-Up Activities: Filling in the Blanks p 28
1. d
2. c
3. e, p
4. i, g, a
5. h
6. m, n
7. f, j
8. k, o
9. l, b

ON THE BUS
Questions about the Picture (*some possible responses*) p 30
1. Ten./ Ten people are waiting at the bus stop./ There are ten people at the bus stop.
2. Baskets, a handbag/ purse, a newspaper.
3. ....

Preview: Filling in the Blanks p 31
1. ticket box
2. picnic basket
3. bus stop
4. bus driver
5. hospital stop
6. traffic light
7. typing lesson
8. rest stop
9. taxi stop
10. notebook

Reading Practice p 31
1. Right.
2. Wrong. (*There's never a bus stop inside a school; maybe in front of/ near/ next to a school.*)
3. Wrong. (*When the traffic light is red, the bus will stop. When it's green, the bus will go.*)
4. Right.
5. Wrong. (*She wants to get on the bus.*)
7. Right.
8. Wrong. (*This depends on the city; there are usually many more bus stops than taxi stops.*)
9. Right. (*Especially on very long trips.*)
10. Wrong. (*The bus driver is at/ in the front of the bus.*)

SLEEPY HEAD
Questions about the Picture (*some possible responses*) p 40
1. At the breakfast table./ In the dining room./ They're at breakfast./ They're at home.
2. Mr. Harris is reading the paper. Mrs. Harris is pouring the coffee. Polly is putting the breakfast/ food on the table./ They're getting ready for breakfast.
3. In bed./ He's in bed.
4. Sleeping./ He's sleeping./ He's dreaming.

Preview: Vocabulary Practice (*some possible responses*) p 41
1. teapot/ tea/ coffee/ milk/ water/ food/ bread/ eggs/ breakfast/ lunch/ *etc.*
2. tea/ milk/ water/ juice/ cocoa/ *etc.*
3. lunch/ dinner/ supper/their food/ *etc.*
4. magazine/ letter/ telegram/ book/ *etc.*
5. lunch/ dinner/ food/ bread/ eggs/ plate/ *etc.*
6. tea pot/ coffee pot/ milk/ food/ *etc.*

Follow-Up Activities (*some possible responses*) p 46
1. e
2. b / c
3. h
4. g
5. handball: e; ice hockey: f; golf: on the golf course; *etc.*
6. b
7. f / b
8. a
9. d
10. diving: in the pool; jumping: in the gymnasium; climbing/ hiking: in the mountains; bicycling/ riding: in the park; *etc.*

Writing Practice: Olympic Games (*some possible responses*) p 46
1.A: boxing/ diving/ gymnastics/ *etc.*

2.C: Australia/ Brazil/ Canada/ *etc.*

3.A: ice hockey/ skating/ skiing/ *etc.*

4.C: Norway/ Sweden/ USA/ *etc.*

5.A: diving/ swimming/ tennis/ *etc.*

6.C: Australia/ Brazil/ Canada/ *etc.*

7.   21/ *etc.*

8.C: Australia/ Brazil/ Canada/ *etc.*

9.B: boxer/ diver/ gymnast/ *etc.*
   (*answer should match with 1.A answer*)

10.C: Australia/ Brazil/ Canada/ *etc.*
   (*answer should match with 2.C answer*)

MR. FIX-IT'S REPAIR SHOP
Questions about the Picture (*some possible responses*) p 48
1. An old man and woman./ I see an old man and an old woman./ I see Mr. and Mrs. Nelson./ *etc.*
2. At home./ They're in their living room./ *etc.*
3. Talking./ They're talking./ He's asking a question./ She's knitting./ Mr. Nelson is looking for something./ She's sitting./ He's standing./ *etc.*

Follow-Up Activities: Filling in the Blanks: Where to Go/What to Pick Up (*some possible responses*) p 54
repair shop: our radio/ a bicycle/ a clock/ a watch/ my uncle's car/ a TV/ *etc.*
(library): a book/ a magazine/ a record/ *etc.*
(theater): two theater tickets/ *etc.*
(pharmacy/drug store): some medicine/ a prescription/ *etc.*
post office: some stamps/ some air-mail envelopes/ a special delivery parcel/ *etc.*
(hospital): my sick friend/ my doctor/ a friend/ a nurse/ *etc.*
(bus station/travel agency): two bus tickets/ a ticket/ *etc.*
(store/shop/market): a notebook/ a book/ paper/ notepaper/ pencils/ *etc.*
flower shop: some flowers/ a bouquet of flowers/ some roses/ a plant/ *etc.*
eye doctor: my glasses/ some eye medicine/ *etc.*

Matching: Expressions p 54
1. h: Now it works!
2. e: Good!
3. d: Darn it!
4. f: I'm sorry.
5. b: It doesn't work.
6. a: Good idea!
7. g: What's the problem?
8. c: I need my glasses.

THE THREE SINGERS
Questions about the Picture (*some possible responses*) p 56
1. The donkey, the cat, and the rooster (cock).
2. They're in front of the farmyard./ They're on (in) the road.
3. A suitcase./ He's carrying his suitcase.
4. The cow, the dog, the duck, and the hen.

Preview: Substitution Practice: What a Beautiful Voice! (*some possible responses*) p 57
What a beautiful animal/ building/ car/ girl/ movie/ story/ *etc.*
What an enormous animal/ building/ car/ submarine/ *etc.*
What an expensive car/ computer/ radio/ submarine/ trip/ *etc.*
What a famous building/ movie/ story/ submarine/ *etc.*
What a fantastic car/ computer/ girl/ man/ movie/ radio/ story /trip/ *etc.*
What a fat animal/ boy/ girl/ man/ *etc.*
What a great building/ car/ computer/ man/ movie/ story/ trip/ *etc.*
What a hungry animal/ boy/ girl/ man/ *etc.*
What a musical animal/ boy/ girl/ man/ *etc.*
What a sleepy animal/ boy/ girl/ man/ *etc.*
What a tall animal/ boy/ building/ girl/ man/ *etc.*
What a thin animal/ boy/ girl/ man/ *etc.*

Follow-Up Activities: Matching: Bilingual Animals p 63

1. cat - e: Meow! Meow!
2. cow - d: Moo! Moo!
3. dog - f: Bow-wow! Bow-wow!
4. donkey - b: Hee-haw! Hee-haw!
5. duck - c: Quack! Quack!
6. hen - g: Cluck! Cluck!
7. rooster - a: Cock-a-doodle-doo!

Scrambled Sentences p 63

1. The three animals never sang in the Big City.
2. Two hens, a cow, and a dog also lived in the farmyard.
3. Roosters don't have beautiful voices, do they?/ Roosters do have beautiful voices, don't they?
4. I don't like to carry heavy suitcases.
5. A donkey is big and strong but a cat isn't./ A cat isn't big and strong but a donkey is.
6. Do you live in a city or on a farm?
7. In some cities there are many cats on the streets./ In many cities there are some cats on the streets.
8. The robbers heard the three animals and ran away.
9. The singing friends carried the three bags of money to the farmyard.
10. The robbers were unhappy but the singers were happy./ The singers were happy but the robbers were unhappy.

THE OPPOSITE FAMILY

Questions about the Picture p 66

1. Mrs. Opposite./ Mrs. Opposite is bringing in the cake./ The mother.
2. Candles./ There are candles on top of the birthday cake.
3. Mr. Opposite./ The father./ The mother./ The person who has a birthday./ *etc.*
4. Yes, he does./ Yes, he looks like his brother.
5. Twelve./ I think they're fourteen years old./ *etc.*

Preview: Vocabulary Practice: Opposites (*some possible responses*) p 67

black: white
awful/ ugly: beautiful/ pretty
new: old
good: bad
happy: unhappy/ sad
short: tall/ long (*a tall boy; a long story*)
asleep: awake
thin: fat
old: young/ new (*a young boy; a new book*)
Hello!: Goodbye!/ Bye!/ So long!
to lose: to find
to open: to close/ to shut
to go: to come/ to return
to turn on: to turn off

Follow-Up Activities: Matching: Birthday Party p 73
1. c
2. g
3. e
4. a
5. d
6. h
7. b
8. f

THE CAT IN THE WINDOW
Questions about the Picture (*some possible responses*) p 76
1. Mr. Moto is in his shop./ He's in front of his antique shop./ He's near the door./ *etc.*
2. They're tourists./ There's a tour group, a mother and her child, and two men./ *etc.*
3. Antiques./ There are antiques for sale in the shop windows./ *etc.*

Preview: Sentence Building: A Doctor's a Person Who ___. (*some possible responses*) p 77
1. An antique dealer's a person who sells valuable old objects.
2. A tourist's someone who likes to travel to interesting places.
3. A tour guide's a man or woman who takes care of tour groups.
4. An archeologist's a person who studies old places and things.
5. A narrator's someone who tells a story/ tells about the characters in a play.
6. Mr. Moto's a dealer who owns an antique shop.
7. A pilot's a person who flies planes or helicopters.
8. A driver's a person who drives a car, taxi, bus or truck.
9. An actor's someone who likes to role play/ take part in a play/ act.
10. A cat's an animal that likes to drink milk.

Follow-Up Activities: Puzzle: The Antique Shop p 82

Across:
1. antiques
5. far
6. in
8. to
9. high
10. rose
11. big
13. Mr. Moto
15. NO
16. L.A.
17. going
19. box
21. begin
22. son
23. lady
24. end
26 window
27. write

Down:
1. archeology
2. tour
3. questions
4. sitting
7. no
9. home
12. go
14. taxi
18. nine
19. bed
20. red
21. B.A.
23. low
25. not